CORE SKILLS

Social Studies

ISBN-13: 978-1-4190-3425-1
ISBN-10:   1-4190-3425-1

The paper used in this book comes from sustainable resources.

Printed in the United States of America.

2 3 4 5 6 7 8   862   14 13 12 11 10 0

D1410635

Steck Vaughn™
A Harcourt Achieve Imprint

www.HarcourtSchoolSupply.com

Contents

Introduction

Social studies focuses on developing knowledge and skill in history, geography, culture, economics, civics, and government. It also focuses on people and their interaction with each other and the world in which they live. *Core Skills: Social Studies* addresses these areas of study and correlates with social studies curriculum throughout the United States. With this book, students can:

- gain a better understanding of their country and its regions
- practice map and geography skills
- work with charts and other graphic devices

The book features 16 chapter lessons on a variety of social studies topics. It also includes:

- interactive questions about the text or pictures
- chapter checkups
- unit skill builders to enhance social studies skills
- unit reviews
- unit tests

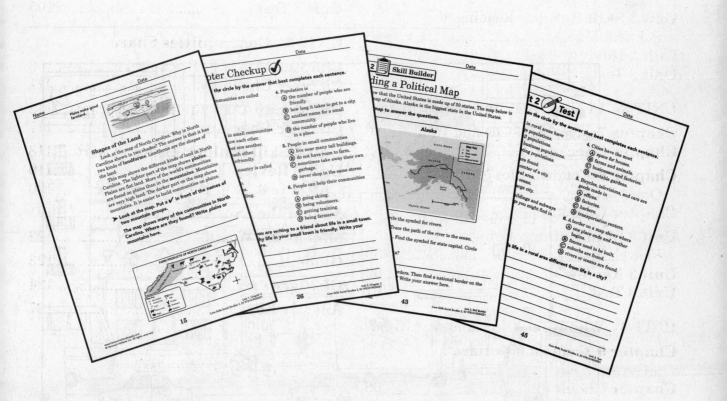

Core Skills Social Studies 3, SV 9781419034251

CHAPTER 1

People and Places

Look at the picture. It shows people in a modern city neighborhood. The people are part of a **community**. A community is a place where people live, work, and play.

People Need Communities

Why do people live in communities? People can help one another when they live together. People also live together so they can get things done. Some people—like you—go to school. Some build roads. Others run stores. One person or one family cannot do all these things alone.

➤ **Think of two reasons why people live in communities. Write your answers here.**

_____

_____

Angela lives
in Santa Fe,
New Mexico.

This is Angela Herrera. She lives in Santa Fe. It is the **capital** of New Mexico. A capital is a city. The government of a U.S. state meets there. New Mexico is one of the 50 states that make up the United States. There are many different communities in each state.

Look at the map below. It shows the state of New Mexico. **Symbols** on the map stand for real things. The **map key** tells what each symbol stands for. A **compass rose** shows directions.

➤ **Find the map key. What does the first symbol stand for? Write your answer here.**

_____

Find the same symbol on the map. Circle it and the city it stands for.

Find the second symbol and circle it on the map.

Circle the compass rose. Is Santa Fe north or south of Albuquerque? Write your answer here.

_____

Many of Santa Fe's buildings look old.

Santa Fe is one of the oldest cities in the United States. It has many beautiful, old buildings. These buildings make Santa Fe different from other U.S. communities. What things make your community different?

Look at the map below. This map shows some buildings in Santa Fe. How does a map show how far apart real places are? The map has a **distance scale**. A distance scale is a measuring line that helps you find distances.

➤ **Find the distance scale in the map key. Circle it.**

Draw a line from the cathedral to the Wheelwright Museum. Use a ruler to measure this line on the distance scale. About how many miles is the cathedral from the museum? Write your answer here.

_____

Buildings are an important part of every community. People work and live and learn in a community's buildings.

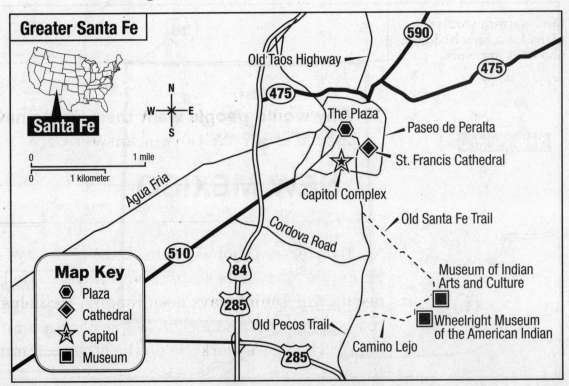

Angela's family likes living in Santa Fe.

Looking at Life in a Community

Here is Angela's family. The Herrerras **depend on** their community for many things. When you depend on something, you put your trust in it. Santa Fe depends on the Herrerra family, too.

Angela's mother works for the city. Her job is to make sure new buildings will not spoil the old look of Santa Fe. Why do you think this job is important to the community?

Mrs. Herrera studies plans for a new building. She likes her work.

➤ **Why would people want their city to have a special look? Write your answer here.**

_____

_____

Mr. Herrera's job is to check the highways in Santa Fe and in the whole state of New Mexico. He helps decide which highways need repairs. He helps keep the roads and streets safe. The people of Santa Fe depend on Mr. Herrera's work. So do the other communities of the state.

Depending on One Another

Angela's family depends on the stores and other **businesses** in the community. A business is a store or other place where people buy and sell things. The Herreras buy the things they need and want from businesses. The businesses depend on people like the Herreras, too. Stores need people to buy the things they sell.

➤ **Look at the pictures. Circle what the Herreras are buying in each picture. Name each place in which the Herreras are buying something. Write your answers on the lines under the pictures.**

_____

_____

_____

Places People Share

People in a community share some places. These are called **public** places. Public places are for everyone to use.

Angela and her family often use the library in Santa Fe. Sometimes they visit the city's parks. Angela goes to a public school in her community, too.

▶ **Find the picture that shows Angela at the library. Circle something in the picture that tells you she is in a library.**

The Herreras often use public places. Angela visits the library.

Angela plays soccer at a public park.

Chapter Checkup ✓

▶ **Darken the circle by the answer that best completes each sentence.**

1. People live, work, and play in a
   - Ⓐ highway.
   - Ⓑ community.
   - Ⓒ business.
   - Ⓓ supermarket.

2. People live together in communities mostly because they
   - Ⓐ like to go to museums.
   - Ⓑ can help one another.
   - Ⓒ want to save old buildings.
   - Ⓓ have to repair highways.

3. The government of a state meets in
   - Ⓐ New Mexico.
   - Ⓑ the largest city.
   - Ⓒ every community.
   - Ⓓ the capital.

4. In this country, every community is one of many in a
   - Ⓐ state.
   - Ⓑ capital.
   - Ⓒ building.
   - Ⓓ museum.

5. People buy what they need from
   - Ⓐ states and capitals.
   - Ⓑ churches and libraries.
   - Ⓒ stores and businesses.
   - Ⓓ cities and towns.

6. Two public places are
   - Ⓐ houses and bands.
   - Ⓑ stores and homes.
   - Ⓒ books and soccer balls.
   - Ⓓ schools and parks.

Thinking & Writing

How do you and your community depend on each other?

_____

_____

_____

_____

_____

_____

_____

CHAPTER 2 Communities and Their Geography

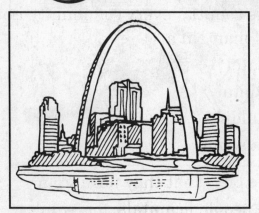

St. Louis is a large city that depends on the Mississippi River in a variety of ways.

Where is your community? Is it in a place that is hilly? Is it in a flat place? Is it by the ocean? Is it hot or cold, rainy or dry?

It is important to know about your community's land and **weather**. Weather is how hot or cold and how wet or dry it is. Weather is an important part of your community.

Riches of the Land

The picture above shows St. Louis, Missouri. St. Louis is on the banks of the Mississippi River. Do you see the river?

➤ **Draw an arrow that points to the Gateway Arch in St. Louis.**

Many communities began along lakes, rivers, and oceans. That's because water is important to communities. People use water in many ways. They drink it, wash with it, and travel on it. They even use it to make electricity and other kinds of power.

➤ **Think of a place in your community where there is water. Write its name here.**

(right) Farming communities grow where the soil is good. (below) Logging communities grow where there are plenty of trees.

There is something else people use water for—fun! People in St. Louis swim in and boat on the Mississippi River. Is there a place in your community where you can do these things?

Water is a **natural resource**. A resource is something people need and use. A natural resource comes from nature. Other natural resources are important to communities, too.

The trees in the picture to the left are in a forest in the western state of Washington. Forests are a natural resource. Wood from the forests is needed by communities all over the country. Is the home you live in made of wood?

Good soil is another natural resource. Do you know why? Farmers need good soil to grow their crops. The food that farmers grow is needed by communities, too.

➤ **What is one natural resource found in your community? Write your answer here.**

_____

Fish are a natural resource, too. In some communities near the sea, people make a living by fishing. The fish are used for food and for other things that people need. Did you know that fish oil is used to make goods such as paint and ink?

▶ **Look at the picture at the top of the page. Circle what the fishermen use to catch the fish.**

Minerals are also natural resources. A mineral is something people get by mining or digging in the ground. Some minerals are rocks, gold, and oil. The picture to the right shows an offshore oil rig. It drills for oil under the sea.

▶ **Name two things that use gas and oil.**

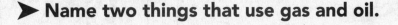

Core Skills Social Studies 3, SV 9781419034251

Rain or Shine

What is the weather like in your community? The kind of weather a place has over a period of time is called **climate**. Climate, like natural resources, is important to communities.

Some communities have mostly sunny and warm weather. One such community is Honolulu, Hawaii. Many people visit Honolulu because of its climate. The city has lots of hotels and restaurants for its visitors.

► **Find the picture of Honolulu below. Circle one natural resource.**

Some communities in Colorado and Utah have lots of snow in the winter. Many people come to these states to ski.

► **Name two kinds of climate that can help a community. Write your answer here.**

_____

_____

The states of Colorado and Utah have a good climate for snow sports.

People enjoy visiting the sunny beaches of Honolulu, Hawaii's largest city.

Plains make good farmland.

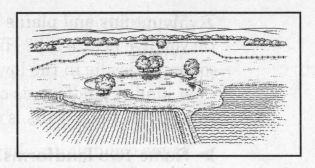

Shapes of the Land

Look at the map of North Carolina. Why is North Carolina shown in two shades? The answer is that it has two kinds of **landforms**. Landforms are the shapes of the land.

This map shows the different kinds of land in North Carolina. The lighter part of the map shows **plains**. Plains are flat land. More of the world's communities are found on plains than in the **mountains**. Mountains are very high land. The darker part on the map shows mountains. It is easier to build communities on plains.

➤ **Look at the map. Put a ✔ in front of the names of two mountain groups.**

The map shows many of the communities in North Carolina. Where are they found? Write *plains* or *mountains* here.

_____

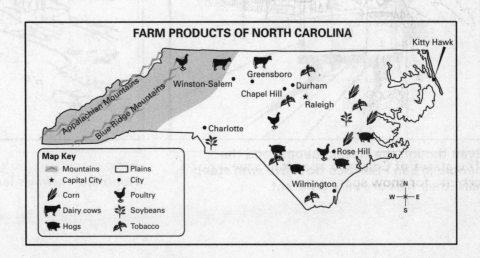

FARM PRODUCTS OF NORTH CAROLINA

Kitty Hawk

Appalachian Mountains

Blue Ridge Mountains

Winston-Salem

Greensboro

Chapel Hill

Durham

★ Raleigh

Charlotte

Rose Hill

Wilmington

Map Key
- ⬜ Mountains
- ★ Capital City
- 🌽 Corn
- 🐄 Dairy cows
- 🐖 Hogs
- ⬜ Plains
- • City
- 🐔 Poultry
- 🌱 Soybeans
- 🍃 Tobacco

N • W • E • S

       Core Skills Social Studies 3, SV 9781419034251

Mountains and plains are two kinds of landforms. Do you live near a hill? Hills are landforms, too. Many communities lie in the low land between mountains. That kind of landform is called a **valley**. A very deep valley with steep walls is called a **canyon**.

➤ **Name two landforms. Write your answer here.**

_____

Landforms make a difference to a community. The work that people do may depend on landforms. The Navajo people of New Mexico and Arizona farm and raise goats and sheep. That's because goats and sheep live well in the hills and canyons of Navajo land.

Landforms can make a difference in other ways, too. San Francisco, California, is a city with many steep hills. It is famous for its cable cars. A cable car is a kind of bus the travels on tracks and goes up and down the hilly streets. Would you like to ride on one?

➤ **Circle the cable car in the picture of San Francisco.**

Even though the Navajo people and the people in San Francisco both live with steep hills, their hills are very different.

Chapter Checkup ✓

➤ **Darken the circle by the answer that best completes each sentence.**

1. Two examples of a water resource are
- Ⓐ mountains and hills.
- Ⓑ lakes and rivers.
- Ⓒ oceans and plains.
- Ⓓ forests and climates.

2. Soil is an important resource for
- Ⓐ loggers.
- Ⓑ skiers.
- Ⓒ sailors.
- Ⓓ farmers.

3. Two mineral resources are
- Ⓐ gold and oil.
- Ⓑ sun and flowers.
- Ⓒ snow and gas.
- Ⓓ fish and rocks.

4. The weather over a period of time is called
- Ⓐ a landform.
- Ⓑ a valley.
- Ⓒ a mineral.
- Ⓓ the climate.

5. Most communities are found on
- Ⓐ hills.
- Ⓑ mountains.
- Ⓒ plains.
- Ⓓ rivers.

6. A landform that is low land between mountains is called a
- Ⓐ plain.
- Ⓑ valley.
- Ⓒ hill.
- Ⓓ canyon.

Thinking & Writing

Why do you think most communities are built on plains? What special problems might communities in mountains have?

_____

_____

_____

_____

_____

_____

Name _____   Date _____

Using a Landform Map

➤ **The map below shows the state of Washington.**
  Use the map key to answer these questions.

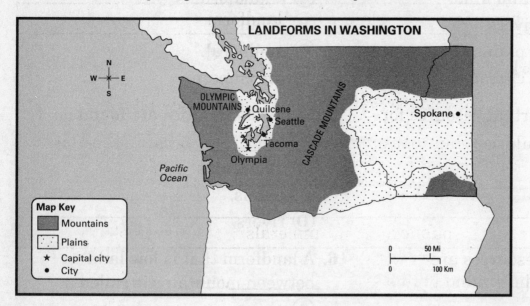

LANDFORMS IN WASHINGTON

N W E S

OLYMPIC MOUNTAINS

Quilcene

Seattle

Tacoma

Olympia

Pacific Ocean

CASCADE MOUNTAINS

Spokane

Map Key
- ▨ Mountains
- ⬚ Plains
- ★ Capital city
- • City

0   50 Mi
0   100 Km

1. What are the two main kinds of landforms
   in Washington?

Plains

_____

2. Find the picture on this page that shows plains.
   Draw a line from the picture of the plains to the
   plains shown on the map. Mark the mountains
   on the map with an <u>M</u>.

Mountains

_____

3. What is the capital of Washington?

_____

4. What does the land look like around Spokane?

_____

Name _____ Date _____

Unit 1  Review

➤ **Each sentence below has a word missing. Choose the missing word for each sentence from the words in the boxes. Then write the words in the correct places on the puzzle.**

ACROSS | business   plain   landform   community

1. People live, work, and play in a _____.

2. A _____ buys or sells things that people need and want.

3. It is easy to build communities on a _____ because it is flat.

4. A _____ is a certain shape of the land.

DOWN | public   minerals   symbol

5. People dig in the ground to find _____.

6. Everyone can use a _____ place.

7. A _____ on a map stands for something real.

Core Skills Social Studies 3, SV 9781419034251

Unit 1  Test

➤ **Darken the circle by the answer that best completes each sentence.**

1. State capitals are cities where
   Ⓐ businesspeople always meet.
   Ⓑ government leaders meet.
   Ⓒ only librarians work.
   Ⓓ all schoolteachers train.

2. Schools and parks are
   Ⓐ public places.
   Ⓑ businesses.
   Ⓒ natural resources.
   Ⓓ landforms.

3. On a map, a compass rose shows
   Ⓐ capitals.
   Ⓑ highways.
   Ⓒ directions.
   Ⓓ distances.

4. Businesses in a community
   Ⓐ clean city parks.
   Ⓑ have books for people to borrow.
   Ⓒ run museums.
   Ⓓ sell things people need.

5. Natural resources include
   Ⓐ climate and communities.
   Ⓑ forests and lakes.
   Ⓒ businesses and stores.
   Ⓓ schools and libraries.

6. Canyons and plains are kinds of
   Ⓐ weather.
   Ⓑ mountains.
   Ⓒ minerals.
   Ⓓ landforms.

Why are natural resources important to communities? Give an example.

_____

_____

_____

_____

_____

_____

_____

CHAPTER 3 Small Communities

Do you live in a small community? If you do, you know one important thing about small communities. In small towns, most people know one another.

Friends and Neighbors

People in small communities see one another a lot. They often shop in the same stores. They buy gas at the same station. They keep money in the same bank. Sometimes they work at the same kinds of jobs.

The picture below shows a small fishing town. People here like to go to the **docks** when the fishing boats come in. The docks are platforms built over the water. Boats load and unload at the docks.

➤ **Circle a dock in the picture.**

Many people in fishing communities depend on the sea.

It is easy to be friendly in a small town. People stop to say hello and to talk. They ask about friends, family, work, and other things. They tell each other the news.

➤ **Put a ✔ on a store shown in the picture.**

Circle something one of the people has just bought in a store.

Put an X on something in the picture that helps people get around their community.

In a small town, it is easy to know many people.

Core Skills Social Studies 3, SV 9781419034251

The Miller family sorts fruits and vegetables by size and puts them into boxes.

Working in Small Communities

Many small towns are in **rural** areas. These are places in the country. These places are not cities.

The Miller family lives in Rose Hill, North Carolina. The **population** of Rose Hill is very small. Population is the number of people that live in a place.

Like their neighbors, the Millers are farmers. They raise turkeys, cattle, and hogs. They also grow watermelons and sweet potatoes. The Millers need a lot of land for their animals and crops. They could not farm in a city.

➤ **Look at the picture of the Millers' fruit stand. Circle what the Millers have grown. Think about their crops. Draw some more things in the fruit stand they might grow. Then explain why you cannot raise cattle in the city. Write your answer here.**

_____

_____

_____

Working Together

People in a small town work together to run their community. Many grown-ups may belong to the fire department. Whenever there is a fire, these people stop the work they are doing and rush to help. This is called a **volunteer** fire department. Volunteers are people who are not paid for the work they do.

People in a small community may also take their own garbage away. This way, the community does not have to pay workers to collect the garbage.

➤ **Why would a community use volunteer workers? Write your answer here.**

_____

_____

A volunteer fire department puts out another fire.

➤ For Your Information

Names of Small Towns

Some small towns in the United States have amazing names! Have you ever heard of Sopchoppy or Moosup? They are both U.S. towns. Sopchoppy is in Florida. Moosup is in Connecticut.

These towns aren't the only ones with unusual names. Some people in Idaho live in a community called Chubbuck. Shinglehouse is a small town in Pennsylvania. Rocky Boy, Montana, is another small town.

➤ **Look at the map. Circle these communities: Sugar Land, Paw Paw, and Winter.**

Find two more communities with unusual names on the map. Write the names here.

_____

_____

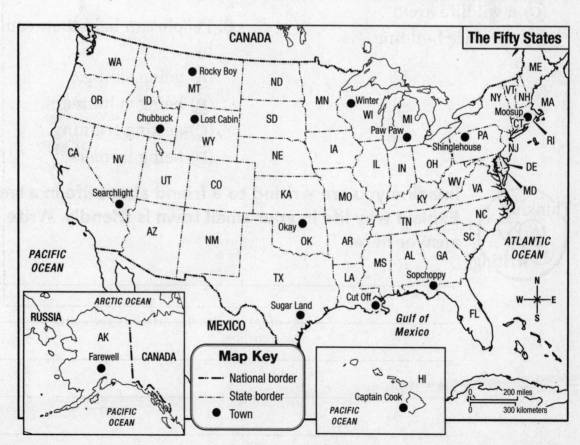

128423

Chapter Checkup ✓

➤ **Darken the circle by the answer that best completes each sentence.**

1. Small communities are called
- Ⓐ cities.
- Ⓑ rural.
- Ⓒ states.
- Ⓓ towns.

2. Most people in small communities
- Ⓐ do not know each other.
- Ⓑ do not greet one another.
- Ⓒ often see each other.
- Ⓓ often act unfriendly.

3. An area in the country is called
- Ⓐ a rural area.
- Ⓑ a town dump.
- Ⓒ a wildlife area.
- Ⓓ an office building.

4. Population is
- Ⓐ the number of people who are friendly.
- Ⓑ how long it takes to get to a city.
- Ⓒ another name for a small community.
- Ⓓ the number of people who live in a place.

5. People in small communities
- Ⓐ live near many tall buildings.
- Ⓑ do not have room to farm.
- Ⓒ sometimes take away their own garbage.
- Ⓓ never shop in the same stores.

6. People can help their communities by
- Ⓐ going skiing.
- Ⓑ being volunteers.
- Ⓒ getting training.
- Ⓓ being farmers.

Imagine you are writing to a friend about life in a small town. Explain why life in your small town is friendly. Write your answer here.

_____

_____

_____

_____

CHAPTER 4 Suburban Communities

Many U.S. citizens live in **suburbs**. A suburb is a community near a big city. Some suburbs can be cities themselves. But suburbs are always near a larger city.

Living in a Suburb

The picture shows Forest Park, Georgia. It is a suburb near Atlanta. The Griffins live here. Most suburbs have homes like the ones in Forest Park. The houses and apartment buildings have yards. Many homes have garages and driveways.

Like many people who live in suburbs, Mrs. Griffin works in the city nearby. She works at the Atlanta airport.

► **Look at the picture. How is this suburb different from a small community? Write your answer here.**

_____

_____

Most suburbs are quiet and peaceful.

There are many reasons why the Griffins like Forest Park. They think the big city is too crowded and noisy. In Forest Park, the streets are quiet. There's a shopping center nearby. But the Griffins like being near the city, too. They can work and have fun in Atlanta.

There are more reasons why the Griffins like Forest Park. The suburb is close to the city, but it feels like a small town. The family has lots of friends and neighbors who live in the community. The Griffins like the schools, too. Both Lavon and Cedric Griffin walk to a school in their own neighborhood. And there's enough room for Mrs. Griffin's garden!

➤ **Look at the picture. Find two things the Griffins like about suburbs. Write your answer here.**

_____

_____

People in suburbs take care of their yards.

Most people in suburbs travel by car.

Getting Around in Suburbs

In suburbs a lot of land is used for homes. Land is also used for roads. It can be a long way from one end of a suburb to another! So people who live in suburbs need to use **transportation**. Transportation is how people or things get from place to place. Most people in suburbs use cars for transportation.

Many people drive to work. Mrs. Griffin drives from Forest Park to Atlanta. People also need cars to go shopping, to visit the doctor, or to go to the movies.

➤ **Name a form of transportation shown in the picture.**

The Kwans enjoy their home in Union City.

The Kwan family lives in Union City. It is a suburb of San Francisco, California. The Kwans live there because it is quieter than San Francisco. In Union City, the Kwans can afford to own a house.

When the Kwans go to San Francisco, they take trains. The trains link San Francisco with the communities around it. Trains link many suburbs to nearby cities.

➤ **Find the compass rose on the map below. The long lines on the compass rose show the main directions. The four short lines stand for in-between directions. For example, the direction between north and east is northeast.**

Find San Francisco on the map. Then find Union City. Draw a line from San Francisco to Union City.

Draw a line under the name of a community southwest of Union City.

Put a ✔ in front of the name of a community northwest of Union City.

Chapter Checkup ✔

▶ **Darken the circle by the answer that best completes each sentence.**

1. A suburb is a
  Ⓐ small fishing village.
  Ⓑ community outside a city.
  Ⓒ kind of shopping center.
  Ⓓ rural community.

2. Many people in suburbs work
  Ⓐ in nearby cities.
  Ⓑ at cutting down trees.
  Ⓒ at busy airports.
  Ⓓ in Union City.

3. The land in suburbs is used mostly for
  Ⓐ offices and trains.
  Ⓑ camping and hiking.
  Ⓒ roads and houses.
  Ⓓ farms and gardens.

4. Most houses in suburbs have
  Ⓐ elevators.
  Ⓑ yards.
  Ⓒ trains.
  Ⓓ airports.

5. The way people get from one place to another is called
  Ⓐ fishing.
  Ⓑ transportation.
  Ⓒ suburbs.
  Ⓓ maps.

6. Most people get from place to place in suburbs by
  Ⓐ bus.
  Ⓑ train.
  Ⓒ plane.
  Ⓓ car.

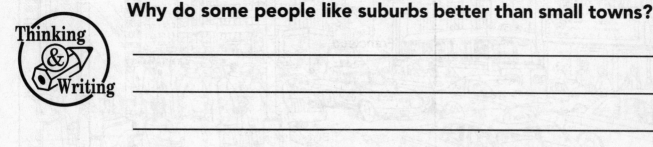

Why do some people like suburbs better than small towns?

_____

_____

_____

_____

_____

_____

_____

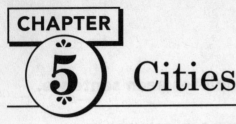

Cities

What makes a city different from a town? Its size, that's what! A city is much bigger than a town. Many people live and work in cities.

Cities Are Big

The picture shows a big city. Millions of people live there. There are many very tall buildings in this city. People work in some of those buildings. Families live in tall buildings, too. There just isn't enough room for everyone to have a house. So, many people in cities live in apartments in tall buildings. All communities have buildings, but cities have many more.

▶ **Put a ✔ by something in the picture you cannot see in a rural community.**

With their skyscrapers, offices, and homes, cities cover a lot of land.

Most cities have an area that is used mostly for business. This area is often called "downtown." People go downtown to work in big office buildings and to shop.

Look at the map of downtown Danville below. Find the area of the city near the ocean. Cities by the water often have a **harbor**. A harbor is a safe place for ships. There, big ships load and unload.

➤ **Put an <u>X</u> on the part of the map that shows the harbor.**

What direction would you travel to get from the stores on Park Lane to the bridge over Cantwell River?

The ships take things made in the city to other communities. They also bring food and other things to the city. In cities, a lot of buildings cover the land. So there is no room to grow food.

➤ **Trace the shortest route from the warehouses on Water Street to the Bruce Street Apartments.**

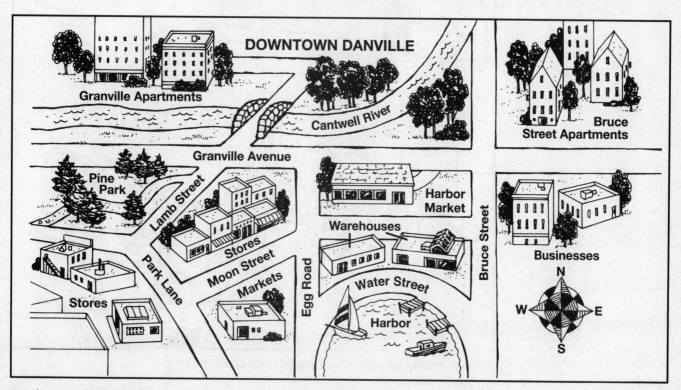

DOWNTOWN DANVILLE

Granville Apartments

Cantwell River

Bruce Street Apartments

Granville Avenue

Pine Park

Lamb Street

Park Lane

Stores

Moon Street

Markets

Stores

Egg Road

Harbor Market

Warehouses

Water Street

Harbor

Bruce Street

Businesses

N
W   E
S

Working in Cities

People in cities work at many different kinds of jobs. Some people sell things in stores. Others unload the ships that come into the harbor. Still others write books or work on newspapers. Do you like to watch television? People who work for television usually work in cities, too.

Many cities have buildings called **factories** where things are made. Things made by people are called **goods**. Toys, pencils, and washing machines are all goods that people make in factories. Can you think of other goods that people make? Chances are they are made in a city.

➤ **Circle what is being made in the picture.**

It takes many people working together to make goods in factories.

34

The Gilder family enjoys going to hear music.

Living in a City

The Gilder family lives in Austin, Texas. Austin is the capital of Texas. Mr. and Mrs. Gilder both work in the city.

The whole family likes to have fun in Austin. Like most cities, Austin has many things to do. The Gilders can go places to hear music. They can see plays and movies.

The family can even watch a football game. Do you have a favorite team? Many cities have sports teams.

Cities also have parks. At a city park, you can have a picnic, ride your bike, play volleyball, or take a walk.

➤ **Name one way the Gilders can have fun in Austin. Write your answer here.**

_____

Chapter Checkup ✓

➤ **Darken the circle by the answer that best completes each sentence.**

1. Many people in cities live in
   (A) factories.
   (B) museums.
   (C) farmhouses.
   (D) apartments.

2. The downtown part of a city is mostly
   (A) for business.
   (B) for living.
   (C) for airports.
   (D) for parks.

3. In cities, the land is used mainly for
   (A) farming.
   (B) subways.
   (C) buildings.
   (D) suburbs.

4. When ships come to cities, they unload at a
   (A) factory.
   (B) subway.
   (C) park.
   (D) harbor.

5. Buildings where things are made are called
   (A) apartments.
   (B) subways.
   (C) factories.
   (D) harbors.

6. Two goods made in factories are
   (A) fish and trees.
   (B) toys and cars.
   (C) turkeys and pigs.
   (D) clothes and cats.

Thinking & Writing

Imagine you live in a big city. Tell why you think the city is special and exciting. Write your answer here.

_____

_____

_____

_____

_____

_____

CHAPTER 6 Your Own Community

You have read about three kinds of communities. In this chapter, you will look at the community where you live.

Different Places

The pictures below show how the land is used in different kinds of communities.

➤ **Look at the pictures. Put a ✔ under the picture that shows a city.**

Put an X under the picture that shows a small town.

Draw a line under the picture that shows a suburb.

Circle the community that is most like the place where you live.

Your **address** tells where you live.

➤ **Write your name and address here.**

_____

_____

_____

A **political map** can tell where you live, too. This one of the United States shows states and their **borders**. A border is a line that shows where one place ends and another place begins.

➤ **Find your state on the map. Circle it.**

Mexico is the country south of the United States. Write the name of a state that is on the border with Mexico.

_____

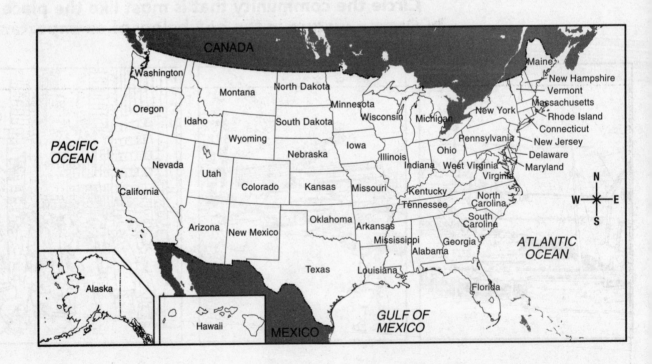

Finding Out

It does not matter whether your community is large or small. There are still many things to learn about it.

What do you know about your community? What would you like to know? Here is a list of questions that one class made.

1. What are some special places to visit?

2. What natural resources do we have?

3. What goods do we make? What crops do we grow?

4. Who is our community proud of?

5. How can we help our community?

➤ **Think of a question of your own to write here.**

_____

_____

➤ **Draw a picture in the box below of an important place in your community.**

39

Many people have office jobs.

Start to find out about your community by asking questions. Talk to people who work in your community. Begin with your family. Find out about their jobs. Do they make things? Do they sell things? Do people in your family grow things or help others? Do they work for pay, or do they volunteer?

To learn more about your community, you will need to do some hunting. A good place to look is the public library. Take a list of questions with you.

➤ **To begin your list, write a question here.**

Take a notebook, too. You may find books in the library about your state and about your community. If you don't, or if you need help, you can ask a librarian.

At the library, you can learn all about your community.

Old pictures can tell you about the past, too. You can find plenty of pictures at the library. This picture shows what cars looked like many years ago. Your community probably looked very different at one time, too!

➤ **Look at the picture. Circle one kind of transportation that people used in the past.**

How can you tell this photograph is old? Write your answer here.

_____

_____

Chapter Checkup ✔

➤ Darken the circle by the answer that best completes each sentence.

1. Three kinds of communities are
   Ⓐ towns, cities, and subways.
   Ⓑ streets, towns, and suburbs.
   Ⓒ towns, suburbs, and cities.
   Ⓓ cities, streets, and countries.

2. A political map helps you
   Ⓐ do your work.
   Ⓑ find out where places are.
   Ⓒ learn to add and subtract.
   Ⓓ look up books.

3. On a map, you can tell where a state ends because of its
   Ⓐ borders.
   Ⓑ oceans.
   Ⓒ resources.
   Ⓓ crops.

4. You can find facts about your community
   Ⓐ in a hospital.
   Ⓑ in the public library.
   Ⓒ in a city.
   Ⓓ from a sports team.

5. Another way to learn about your community is to
   Ⓐ play ball.
   Ⓑ go shopping.
   Ⓒ go on a long trip.
   Ⓓ ask people questions.

6. You can learn about life long ago through
   Ⓐ your address.
   Ⓑ old pictures.
   Ⓒ new buildings.
   Ⓓ new pictures.

Thinking & Writing

Is your community a small town, a suburb, or a city? Explain your choice. Write your answer here.

_____

_____

_____

_____

_____

Unit 2 | Skill Builder

Reading a Political Map

You know that the United States is made up of 50 states. The map below is a political map of Alaska. Alaska is the biggest state in the United States.

▶ **Use the map to answer the questions.**

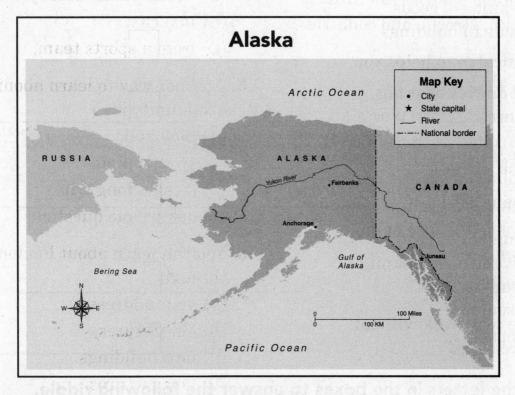

Alaska

Map Key
- • City
- ★ State capital
- — River
- —·—·— National border

Arctic Ocean

RUSSIA

ALASKA

Yukon River • Fairbanks

CANADA

Anchorage•

Bering Sea

Gulf of Alaska

Juneau

0 _____ 100 Miles
0 _____ 100 KM

Pacific Ocean

1. Look at the map key. Circle the symbol for rivers.

2. Find a river on the map. Trace the path of the river to the **ocean.**

3. Look at the map key again. Find the symbol for state capital. Circle Alaska's capital.

4. What ocean is north of Alaska?

_____

5. Find the symbol for national borders. Then find a national border on the map. What nation's border is it? Write your answer here.

_____

Unit 2  Review

▶ **Use a word from the box to complete each sentence below. Write the word on the lines next to each sentence.**

| suburbs | population | transportation | volunteers | factories |

1. Many kinds of goods are made in buildings called _____.

___ ___ ___ ___ ___ [ ] ___ ___ ___

2. Communities near big cities are _____.

___ [ ] ___ ___ ___ ___ ___

3. People or things get from place to place by means of _____.

___ ___ ___ ___ ___ ___ [ ] ___ ___ ___ ___ ___

4. The number of people who live in a community make up its _____.

___ ___ ___ ___ ___ [ ] ___ ___ ___ ___

5. People who work without pay are called _____.

___ ___ ___ [ ] ___ ___ ___ ___ ___ ___

▶ **Use the letters in the boxes to answer the following riddle.**

Riddle: If you're a farmer, you live in this kind of area.

Answer: ___ ___ ___ ___ ___

Unit 2 Test

➤ **Darken the circle by the answer that best completes each sentence.**

1. Towns in rural areas have
  Ⓐ large populations.
  Ⓑ small populations.
  Ⓒ only business populations.
  Ⓓ no voting populations.

2. Suburbs are found
  Ⓐ in the center of a city.
  Ⓑ in a rural area.
  Ⓒ near an ocean.
  Ⓓ near a large city.

3. Tall office buildings and subways are two things you might find in
  Ⓐ suburbs.
  Ⓑ cities.
  Ⓒ towns.
  Ⓓ harbors.

4. Cities have the most
  Ⓐ space for houses.
  Ⓑ farms and animals.
  Ⓒ businesses and factories.
  Ⓓ vegetable gardens.

5. Bicycles, televisions, and cars are goods made in
  Ⓐ offices.
  Ⓑ factories.
  Ⓒ harbors.
  Ⓓ transportation centers.

6. A border on a map shows where
  Ⓐ one place ends and another begins.
  Ⓑ fences need to be built.
  Ⓒ suburbs are found.
  Ⓓ rivers or oceans are found.

Thinking & Writing

How is life in a rural area different from life in a city?

_____

_____

_____

_____

_____

_____

CHAPTER 7

Meeting Needs and Wants

This morning you woke up and put on your clothes. Clothes are things that everyone needs. Then you had breakfast. People also need food to live. You did all of this in your home. Everyone needs a place to live. This place is called **shelter**. Food, clothes, and shelter are **needs** for everyone in a community. Needs are things you must have in order to live.

Why People Work

People work to meet their needs. They use the money they earn to buy what they need. People also use money to buy their **wants**. Wants are things you would like to have. You don't need these things to live.

➤ **The woman in the picture is buying flowers for her home. Are flowers a want or a need? Write *want* or *need* here.**

_____

The woman uses the money she makes to buy things she needs and wants.

Look at the pictures below. In the first picture, the boy is making something.

➤ Circle the tool the boy is using.

In the second picture, the boy is selling what he has made. A person who grows or makes things for sale is a **producer**. Producers make money.

➤ Show that the boy is a producer. Write *producer* below the second picture.

Now look at the third picture. How is the boy spending his money? When people make money, they can spend it for something that they want or need. A person who buys something to eat or to use is a **consumer**. Consumers spend money.

➤ Show that the boy is a consumer. Write *consumer* below the third picture.

People Need Services

Do you take your clothes to a cleaner? Have you ever been to the dentist for a checkup? Who do you visit to get your hair cut? If you have done any of these things, you have used a **service**. A service is something people do that other people need or want.

Services are one reason people live together in communities. Different people can do different work. If you lived all by yourself, you would have to do everything yourself. You would not have time for anything else.

Look at the picture below. The doctor is performing a service. She is giving the boy a checkup.

➤ **Circle the person who is giving the service.**

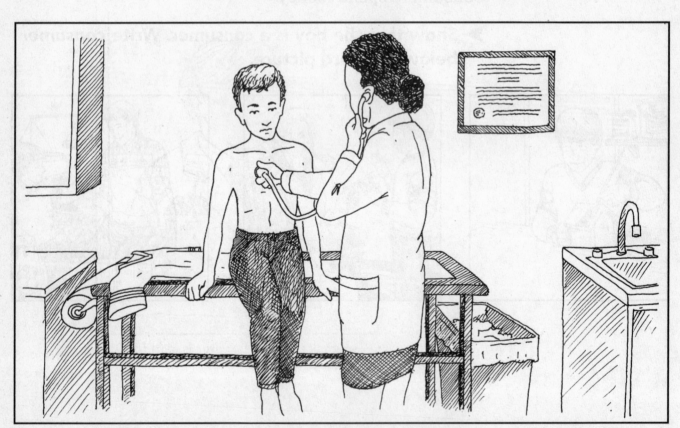

The doctor is performing a service. She is giving the boy a checkup.

Look at the picture below. The worker is checking the community's water to make sure it is safe to drink. This is a service that communities provide. Later you will learn more about other services that communities offer.

People who work for the community make money for doing their jobs. They use the money they earn to buy food, clothes, and other things.

➤ **Why is it important for a community to have clean water? Write your answer here.**

_____

_____

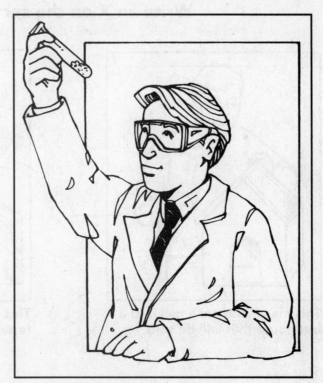

Workers make sure that water is safe for the community.

Today, more people than ever work in service jobs. In 1900, almost one out of every two people farmed. Now, most people have service jobs. More than twice as many people have this kind of job as any other kind.

People who repair computers or shoes or cars are service workers. So are nurses, teachers, and lawyers. Service workers are also the people who run hotels and work in television and the movies. Think about the people you know. How many of them are service workers?

➤ **Look at the pictures below. Label the producer. Circle what the person is producing.**

Write an X on the service worker.

This man hammers a nail into a birdhouse that will be sold.

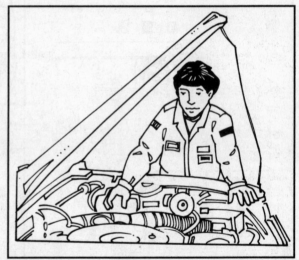

This man looks under the car's hood to repair the car.

Come to the street fair!

➤ Look at the picture below. Circle two people who are service workers.

Put an **X** on three consumers.

What are two things you can buy at this fair?
Write your answer here.

_____

Chapter Checkup ✓

➤ **Darken the circle by the answer that best completes each sentence.**

1. Three needs people have are
   Ⓐ food, shelter, and clothes.
   Ⓑ services, toys, and homes.
   Ⓒ movies, money, and fairs.
   Ⓓ barbers, records, and cleaners.

2. A want is something
   Ⓐ you need to live.
   Ⓑ you make yourself.
   Ⓒ you do not need to live.
   Ⓓ producers use to make things.

3. A producer is someone who
   Ⓐ pays for things.
   Ⓑ uses things.
   Ⓒ makes things.
   Ⓓ needs things.

4. When you buy something to eat, you are a
   Ⓐ teacher.
   Ⓑ consumer.
   Ⓒ builder.
   Ⓓ producer.

5. When you go to a dentist, you are
   Ⓐ doing a job.
   Ⓑ getting a haircut.
   Ⓒ working for money.
   Ⓓ using a service.

6. Workers pay for their needs with
   Ⓐ tickets.
   Ⓑ money.
   Ⓒ doctors.
   Ⓓ shelter.

Thinking & Writing

Write about one of your wants. Explain why it is a want and not a need.

_____

_____

_____

_____

_____

_____

_____

Communities Need One Another

What did you wear to school today? Your clothes might have come from a store in your community. But they were probably made somewhere else. No community makes and grows everything it needs.

Goods from Many Communities

The things you need and want come from many different communities. (Remember that things that are made by people are called **goods**.) Some goods arrive by airplane. Others arrive by train. How many different kinds of cars do you see on the train? Each one carries something different. What could be in those train cars? Maybe this train is headed for your community.

➤ **How else can goods get to your community? Write your answer here.**

_____

_____

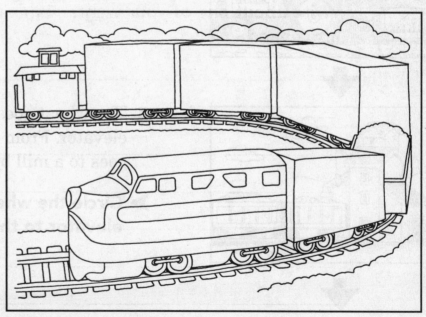

Many goods are carried to places by train.

Making Bread

Have you ever made bread? If so, you know there are many steps in making it. A **flowchart** shows the step-by-step order in which something is done. This flowchart shows all the steps in making bread. It takes many people in many communities to make the bread you buy in a store. Read each step. Then follow the arrow to the next step.

1. A farmer plants the seeds to grow wheat.

➤ **Put an X on two natural resources that help the farmer grow wheat.**

2. When the wheat is ready, it is cut.

3. The wheat goes by truck to a grain elevator. From the elevator, the wheat goes to a mill by train.

➤ **Circle the wheat going from the elevator to the train.**

4. Workers in the mill wash, dry, and crush the wheat. Then they make it into flour.

► **Circle the bags of flour that come from the mill.**

5. Next, the flour goes from the mill to the bakery.

► **What kind of transportation is used? Write your answer here.**

_____

6. Bakers make dough from the flour and bake the bread in hot ovens. Mmmm! Then the bread is sliced and wrapped.

7. Now the bread is on its way to other communities.

► **Circle the place where the driver takes the bread.**

8. The bread goes onto shelves.

► **What happens next? Write your answer here.**

_____

► **Circle two people who work in the store.**

Unit 3, Chapter 8
Core Skills Social Studies 3, SV 9781419034251

A Chain of Workers

Many workers help get bread to your community. It takes many workers to get most things to your stores. The workers form a kind of chain. If workers in one community do not do their jobs, the chain breaks.

➤ **Look at the flowchart below. Put a ✔ under the first worker in the chain.**

Put an X under the worker who makes sure the milk is heated.

Circle the worker who delivers the milk.

People depend on other workers for their jobs. If the farmer doesn't milk the cows, then the other workers cannot do their jobs.

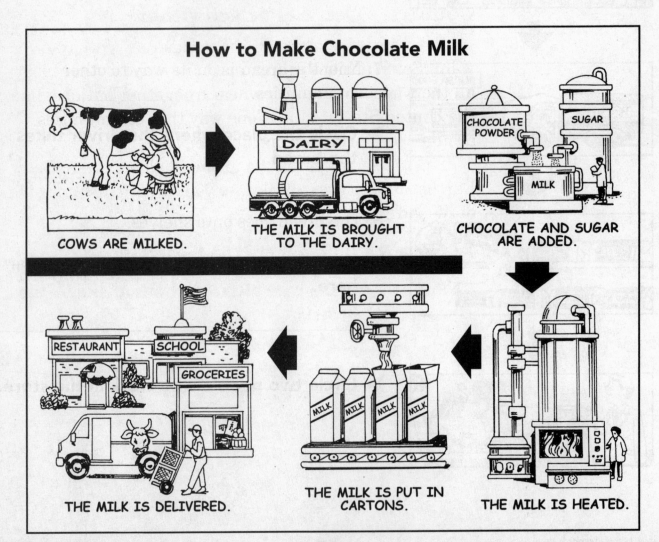

How to Make Chocolate Milk

COWS ARE MILKED.

THE MILK IS BROUGHT TO THE DAIRY.

CHOCOLATE AND SUGAR ARE ADDED.

THE MILK IS DELIVERED.

THE MILK IS PUT IN CARTONS.

THE MILK IS HEATED.

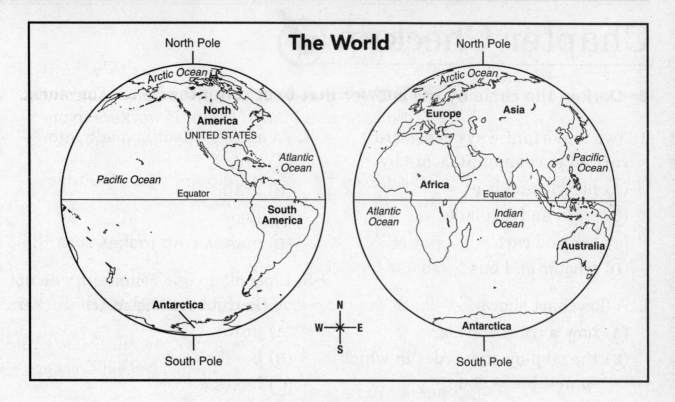

The World

North Pole

Arctic Ocean

North America

UNITED STATES

Atlantic Ocean

Pacific Ocean

Equator

South America

Antarctica

South Pole

North Pole

Arctic Ocean

Europe   **Asia**

Pacific Ocean

Africa

Equator

Atlantic Ocean   *Indian Ocean*

Australia

Antarctica

South Pole

N
W — E
S

Countries Can Help Each Other

Few countries make all the things they need and want. Some nations in Asia can't grow enough food for all their needs. They buy wheat from other nations, like the United States. This is one way that communities around the world help one another.

Look at the pictures of a **globe**. A globe is a model of Earth. The pictures are flat, so you can see just one side of the globe at a time.

➤ **Circle the United States on the left globe.**

Put an <u>X</u> on the part of the globe that shows the continent of Asia.

Chapter Checkup ✓

➤ **Darken the circle by the answer that best completes each sentence.**

1. Two important ways goods are carried to communities are by
   - (A) bicycle and boat.
   - (B) train and airplane.
   - (C) car and cart.
   - (D) tractor and bus.

2. A flowchart shows
   - (A) how a train travels.
   - (B) the step-by-step order in which something is done.
   - (C) the way farmers cut wheat.
   - (D) how to find countries on a map.

3. The first step in making bread is done by a
   - (A) baker.
   - (B) seller.
   - (C) miller.
   - (D) farmer.

4. At a mill, wheat is made into
   - (A) bread.
   - (B) grain.
   - (C) flour.
   - (D) money.

5. If people in one community do not do their jobs, the chain of workers
   - (A) grows.
   - (B) breaks.
   - (C) bakes.
   - (D) buys.

6. You can look at a globe to find out
   - (A) how much bread costs.
   - (B) where milk comes from.
   - (C) where Asia is in the world.
   - (D) how to get to school.

Thinking & Writing

Would you rather be a producer or a service worker? Tell what product you would like to produce or what service you would offer. Explain your reason.

_____

_____

_____

_____

_____

Name _____ Date _____

Using a Flowchart

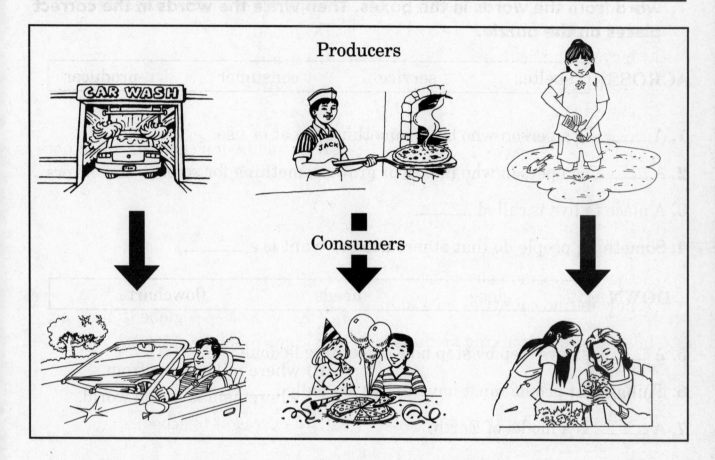

Producers

Consumers

As you know, producers can make goods or services. The flowchart below shows you how producers meet consumers' wants and needs.

1. Circle the producer that offers a service.

2. Underline the consumers who bought something that is a need.

3. Which consumer bought a service? Write your answer here.

_____

4. Did the consumer who bought a service meet a need or a want? Explain your answer.

_____

Name _____ Date _____

➤ **Each of the sentences below has a word missing. Choose the missing word from the words in the boxes. Then write the words in the correct places on the puzzle.**

ACROSS | shelter | service | consumer | producer |

1. A _____ is a person who buys something to eat or use.

2. A _____ is a person who makes or grows something for sale.

3. A place to live is called _____.

4. Something people do that others need or want is a _____.

DOWN | globe | needs | flowchart |

5. A _____ shows step by step how something is done.

6. Things that people must have to live are called _____.

7. A _____ is a model of Earth.

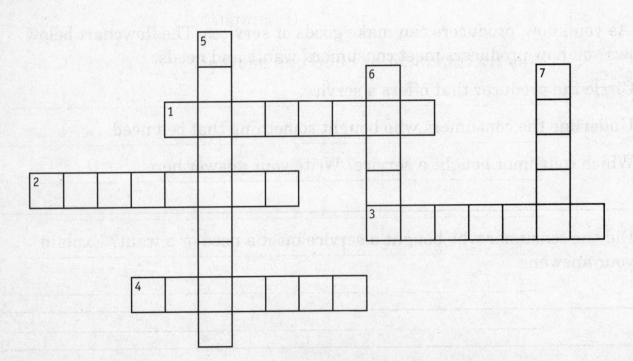

Unit 3  Test

➤ **Darken the circle by the answer that best completes each sentence.**

1. Two needs people have are
   - (A) toys and books.
   - (B) clothes and cars.
   - (C) pets and coats.
   - (D) food and shelter.

2. Most workers today are
   - (A) factory workers.
   - (B) farmers.
   - (C) service workers.
   - (D) construction workers.

3. You are using a service when you
   - (A) buy milk at the grocery store.
   - (B) visit the dentist.
   - (C) get a new bike.
   - (D) buy a birthday present.

4. A consumer
   - (A) is the owner of a farm.
   - (B) makes goods in a factory.
   - (C) buys goods.
   - (D) sells fresh fruit.

5. A flowchart shows
   - (A) how things are connected.
   - (B) the way water moves from place to place.
   - (C) facts about things that move.
   - (D) the step-by-step order in which something is done.

6. A globe is a kind of
   - (A) map.
   - (B) chain.
   - (C) flowchart.
   - (D) graph.

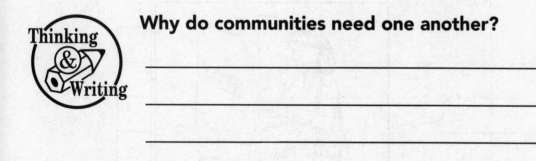

Why do communities need one another?

_____

_____

_____

_____

_____

_____

CHAPTER 9 Communities Have a Government

Have you ever played the game Follow the Leader? If so, you know that the leader is the person who decides what you will do. A community has leaders, too. These leaders help a community make important choices.

Choosing Leaders

People in communities have many different jobs. Some are doctors or teachers. Others are bankers or shopkeepers.

However, each member of a community has to help make choices for the community, too. One way people do this is by voting for leaders to run the community. Voting is a fair way for people to choose their leaders.

➤ **Why is it important for people to vote? Write your answer here.**

_____

_____

Before people vote, they think carefully. They think about the people running for office. Will their ideas be good for the community? Will their ideas be good for me?

When you are older, you will vote for community leaders. Now, you can vote for class leaders. Ms. Carter's students voted for a class leader. You can see the results on the **bar graph**. A bar graph uses bars to stand for numbers. It helps you compare different groups of numbers.

➤ **Read the title and the words at the bottom of each bar. What do the bars show?**

_____

Read the words on the left side of the graph. What do the numbers stand for?

_____

Write the number of votes next to each name. Circle the winner's name.

Brandon _____   **Jenna** _____

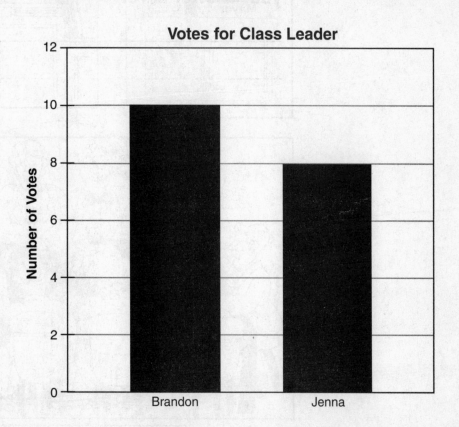

Votes for Class Leader

A Look at Leaders

The leaders who make choices and rules for a community are part of its **government**. A community has three main kinds of leaders in its government. Let's see who they are.

The **lawmakers** make new **laws** or change old ones. Rules for communities are called laws.

The **mayor** is the main leader of the government in many communities. One of the mayor's jobs is to make sure the community's laws are obeyed. Does your community have a mayor?

A **judge** decides if a law has been broken. The place where judges work is a court.

➤ **Look at the pictures. Number the lawmakers 1̲, the mayor 2̲, and the judge 3̲.**

Government Leaders at Work

A mayor tries to solve problems in a community. The mayor works with lawmakers to pass laws that will improve things.

A mayor also tries to make sure that the people in a community get all the services they need. A mayor chooses other people to help provide these services. Can you name the chief of police in your community? The mayor probably chose this person for the job. Look at the **chart** below. A chart presents facts in a way that is easy to read.

► **Circle the person who makes sure that community health laws are not broken.**

The leaders of a community want to make it a good place to live. So they try to be sure that the people in a community follow its laws. Judges decide what to do with people who break the laws.

People Chosen by Mayor	Their Jobs
Fire Chief:	runs the fire department
Police Chief:	runs the police department
Health Inspector:	makes sure that community health laws are not broken
Consumer Protector:	makes sure that laws protecting buyers and sellers are not broken
Building Inspector:	makes sure that buildings meet safety laws

Chapter Checkup ✓

▶ Darken the circle by the answer that best completes each sentence.

1. An important job of a community
   leader is to
   Ⓐ break laws.
   Ⓑ play games.
   Ⓒ make promises.
   Ⓓ make choices.

2. Communities choose leaders by
   Ⓐ thinking.
   Ⓑ building.
   Ⓒ voting.
   Ⓓ writing.

3. Two community leaders people
   vote for are
   Ⓐ mayor and lawmaker.
   Ⓑ doctor and shopkeeper.
   Ⓒ artist and judge.
   Ⓓ banker and teacher.

4. One of the mayor's jobs is to
   Ⓐ decide if a law has been broken.
   Ⓑ make new laws.
   Ⓒ run the fire department.
   Ⓓ provide community services.

5. Judges are community leaders who
   Ⓐ make new laws.
   Ⓑ see that laws are obeyed.
   Ⓒ provide community services.
   Ⓓ decide if laws are broken.

6. The main reason new laws are
   passed in a community is to
   Ⓐ help the police.
   Ⓑ improve things.
   Ⓒ punish people.
   Ⓓ keep courts busy.

Thinking & Writing

Why do communities need leaders? Write your answer here.

_____

_____

_____

_____

_____

Name _____ Date _____

CHAPTER 10

Communities Have Rules and Laws

Have you ever played checkers? Can you name some rules in checkers? Rules help people make choices. Rules tell us what to do or not to do. Rules tell us what is fair, too.

▶ **Look at the picture. Put an X on the girl who is taking her turn.**

Using Rules

Most families have rules. Schools have rules, too. Do you say "thank you" when someone gives you a gift? Many rules are about being polite and kind. You may have learned them from your family, friends, or teachers. Other rules help keep people safe and healthy. Do you have a rule about no running in your school halls? That rule is for safety.

Rules make a game more fun. What happens when someone doesn't follow the rules?

Breaking rules can cause all kinds of problems. Let's see what some might be.

➤ **Put an X on the girl who broke a rule about homework.**

Circle the girl who did not follow a softball rule.

What rule did the boy break when he dropped paper on the playground? Write the rule here.

_____

Rules for Communities

Rules for communities are called laws. You read in Chapter 9 about some of the leaders who make and help keep the laws.

Communities have laws for the same reasons that families, schools, and games have rules. Laws help people make good choices about what is fair. Laws also help the people of a community live and work together.

The signs on this page show some laws in a community.

➤ **Circle the sign that tells people how fast they can drive their cars.**
According to this sign, how fast can people drive?

_____

Find the sign that tells people to stop. Color the sign red.

Laws at Work

Mrs. Kim is getting a ticket. She drove faster than the speed limit allows. Now she will have to pay a fine.

➤ **Look at the picture. Does Mrs. Kim look happy or worried?**

_____

How fast do you think Mrs. Kim was driving? How fast do you think she should drive?

_____

If Mrs. Kim thinks she was not wrong, she can go to traffic court. A judge will hear her side of the story. The judge will decide whether or not Mrs. Kim has broken the law.

Communities have many laws about cars and traffic.

A community has many laws to protect people's health, too. Did you know there are laws that make sure buildings are safe?

Most communities have laws about food and restaurants. By law, every restaurant has to be clean. Inspectors visit every restaurant in the community. They make sure the kitchens are scrubbed clean every day. They check to be sure the food is kept fresh and cold, too.

➤ **Look at the picture below. Why do you think restaurants should be checked?**

_____

_____

People enjoy eating in clean restaurants.

Chapter Checkup ✓

▶ **Darken the circle by the answer that best completes each sentence.**

1. Rules help you make choices and
   Ⓐ hurt people's feelings.
   Ⓑ know what is fair.
   Ⓒ count the population.
   Ⓓ read traffic lights.

2. You learn most rules from
   Ⓐ games, sports, and homework.
   Ⓑ checkups, tickets, and court.
   Ⓒ inspectors, safety, and judges.
   Ⓓ family, friends, and teachers.

3. A community's rules are called
   Ⓐ leaders.
   Ⓑ choices.
   Ⓒ laws.
   Ⓓ votes.

4. Many laws protect people's
   Ⓐ health and safety.
   Ⓑ games and toys.
   Ⓒ languages and signs.
   Ⓓ food and feelings.

5. One example of a safety rule is
   Ⓐ throwing litter on the street.
   Ⓑ taking turns playing a game.
   Ⓒ obeying traffic signals.
   Ⓓ thanking someone for a gift.

6. If you break a law, you may have to
   Ⓐ make a new rule.
   Ⓑ pay a fine.
   Ⓒ visit a restaurant.
   Ⓓ go home.

Thinking & Writing

Think of one rule in your community and explain why you think it is important.

_____

_____

_____

_____

_____

_____

_____

72

CHAPTER 11 Communities Provide Services

You know that some workers provide services. Communities provide services, too. These services help people who live in communities. A school is one example of a service provided by a community.

➤ **Circle the person in the picture who is providing a service.**

What Communities Need

Towns and cities need many services besides schools. All communities need a way to bring water and electricity to everyone who lives there. They need workers to put out fires and to protect people. Communities need roads and buildings, too.

Teachers are community workers.

www.harcourtschoolsupply.com
73
Unit 4, Chapter 11
Core Skills Social Studies 3, SV 9781419034251

Name _____   Date _____

How do communities provide services such as schools? They hire people to build them and work in them. It takes many people with many different skills to do all these jobs.

➤ **Look at the picture. Color the hat of the worker who is hammering.**

Circle the worker who is laying bricks.

Put an X on the inspector who is looking at the plans.

How Communities Pay for Things

Each person who works earns money. Workers pay part of the money they earn to their community. This payment is called a **tax**.

➤ **Look at the flowchart below. Put a ✔ under the box that says WORKERS ARE PAID.**

Circle the box about workers paying taxes.

The community spends tax money to build schools and to pay workers. Tax money helps the community to provide other services, too.

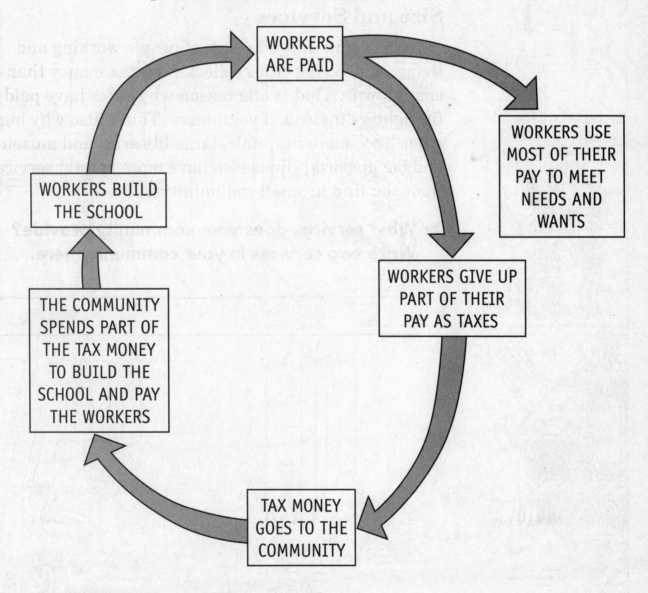

Many cities have busy airports.

Size and Services

A big community has lots of people working and living in it. So big cities collect more tax money than small towns. That is one reason why cities have paid firefighters instead of volunteers. That's also why big cities have more hospitals, large libraries and museums, and big airports. Cities also have more special services than you find in small communities.

➤ **What services does your community provide? Write two services in your community here.**

_____

_____

Communities often provide special services. This community needs help clearing the snow. What kind of weather does your community have?

Sometimes communities, both large and small, need special services. Look at the picture on the left. What weather did this community have?

▶ **What service do the people of this community need when it snows? Write your answer here.**

_____

Another service a community might offer is a consumer department. The workers in a consumer department make sure that consumers get what they pay for. Consumer workers check to see that store owners treat customers fairly.

▶ **Look at the picture. How does this service help people in the community? Write your answer here.**

_____

A city inspector makes sure buildings are safe.

Communities need services for many reasons. The pictures in the left column below show a few of those reasons. The pictures on the right show community workers who can provide the services that will solve the problems shown.

➤ **What is happening in picture A? Draw a line from picture A to the picture of the community worker who can help.**

Draw lines from pictures B, C, and D to the community workers who can solve those problems.

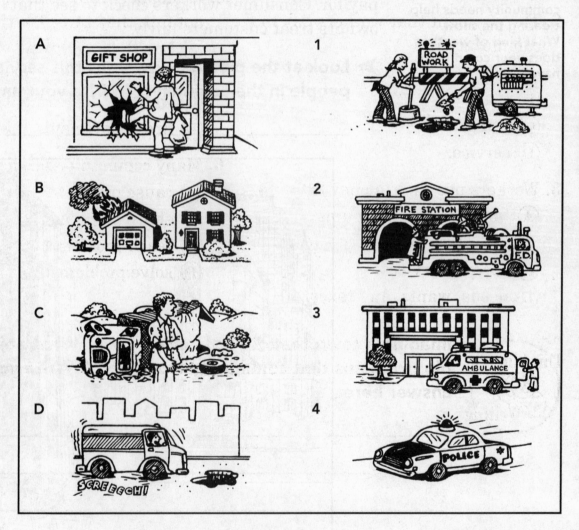

Chapter Checkup ✔

➤ **Darken the circle by the answer that best completes each sentence.**

1. Two services provided by communities are
   - Ⓐ taxes and earnings.
   - Ⓑ barbers and cleaners.
   - Ⓒ schools and firefighting.
   - Ⓓ students and teachers.

2. The payment that workers pay to a community is a
   - Ⓐ gift.
   - Ⓑ tax.
   - Ⓒ want.
   - Ⓓ service.

3. Workers use their money for
   - Ⓐ libraries and museums.
   - Ⓑ volunteer helpers.
   - Ⓒ special services.
   - Ⓓ needs, wants, and taxes.

4. Small communities usually have
   - Ⓐ less tax money than big cities.
   - Ⓑ no tax money.
   - Ⓒ more tax money than big cities.
   - Ⓓ tax money only some years.

5. If shoppers think store owners are not fair, they can go to the
   - Ⓐ health department.
   - Ⓑ consumer department.
   - Ⓒ weather department.
   - Ⓓ fire department.

6. Many community services help
   - Ⓐ cause problems.
   - Ⓑ share problems.
   - Ⓒ teach problems.
   - Ⓓ solve problems.

Thinking & Writing

Imagine a town that did not collect taxes. What are three big problems that community would face? Write your answer here.

_____

_____

_____

_____

_____

_____

Name _____   Date _____

Reading a Bar Graph

➤ **Look at the bar graph below. It shows the <u>census</u> count for the community of Blue Bay. A census is a count of how many people live in a place. Use the graph to answer the questions.**

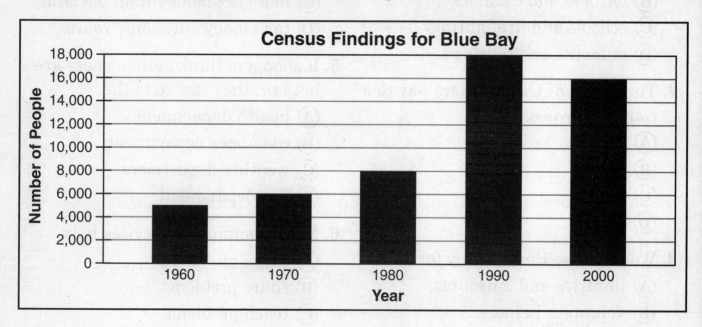

1. How many people lived in Blue Bay in 1960?

_____

2. By what year had the number of people in Blue Bay grown to 18,000?

_____

3. Were more people living in Blue Bay between 1980 and 1990 or between 1970 and 1980?

_____

4. In 1995, a computer company opened in Bell Valley. Between 1995 and 2000, many people in Blue Bay moved to Bell Valley to work. How did this change the 2000 census?

_____

Unit 4  Review

▶ **Use a word from the box to complete each sentence below. Write the word on the lines next to each sentence.**

bar   census   judge   service   government   laws   mayor

1. A community's rules are its _____.

2. A _____ is a count of how many people live in a place.

3. A _____ graph helps you compare different groups of numbers.

4. A _____ decides if a community law has been broken.

5. Members of a _____ make choices and rules for a community.

6. In many communities, the _____ is the main leader.

7. Community workers have _____ jobs.

▶ **Use the letters in the boxes to answer the following riddle.**

Riddle: How are the President of the United States and a mayor alike?

Answer: They are both __ __ __ __ __ __ __.

Unit 4 ✎ Test

➤ Darken the circle by the answer that best completes each sentence.

1. People who make rules for a community are part of its
   - Ⓐ banks.
   - Ⓑ government.
   - Ⓒ courts.
   - Ⓓ police department.

2. The main leader in many communities is the
   - Ⓐ judge.
   - Ⓑ building inspector.
   - Ⓒ fire chief.
   - Ⓓ mayor.

3. Rules help us to
   - Ⓐ be safe and fair.
   - Ⓑ run for office.
   - Ⓒ fight fires.
   - Ⓓ win at softball.

4. People pay taxes for
   - Ⓐ schools and police.
   - Ⓑ business owners and lawmakers.
   - Ⓒ mail carriers and dentists.
   - Ⓓ shopkeepers and students.

5. Community workers have
   - Ⓐ manufacturing jobs.
   - Ⓑ teaching jobs.
   - Ⓒ service jobs.
   - Ⓓ farming jobs.

6. Rules for communities are
   - Ⓐ services.
   - Ⓑ government.
   - Ⓒ promises.
   - Ⓓ laws.

Thinking & Writing

Why is the job of mayor important?

_____

_____

_____

_____

_____

_____

CHAPTER  12 American Indian Communities

The land along the Missouri River is rich and good for farming. But in 1830, only about 2,000 people lived there. They were a group of American Indians called the Omaha. The map below shows where they lived.

The Omaha, like most people, liked living near each other. They lived in villages. Living close together made life safer from attacks.

▶ **About how many miles was it across Omaha land? Write your answer here.**

_____

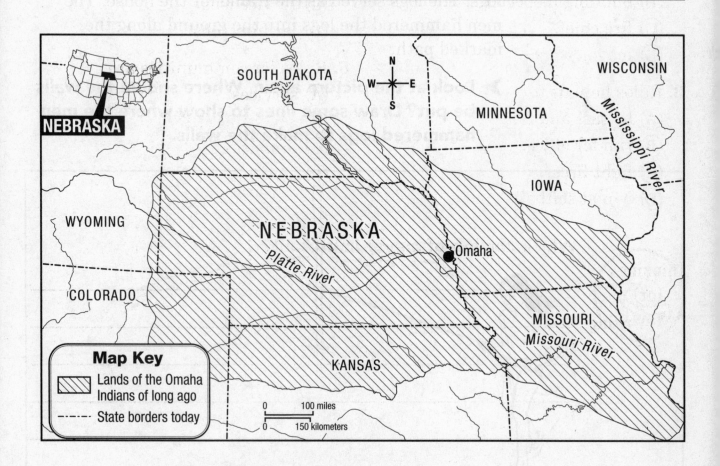

Map Key

▨ Lands of the Omaha Indians of long ago

–·– State borders today

The Omaha built their homes close together. They made them out of the earth itself. These homes were called **earth lodges**. Men and women worked together to make the earth lodges.

The first step was to outline the lodge walls in the dirt. One man did this job. The man took a short, wooden pole and hammered it into the dirt. Then he tied a rope to the top of the pole. He pulled the rope tight. Holding on to the rope, he walked in a circle around the pole. The path he left showed where the wall would be. So he made sure he dragged and shuffled his feet!

➤ **Draw a line to finish the circle on the picture below.**

After the circle was made, a group of men cut heavy logs. The logs served as the frame for the house. The men hammered the logs into the ground along the marked path.

➤ **Look at the picture again. Where should the walls be put? Draw some lines to show where the men hammered logs to make the walls.**

Once the walls were up, the women went to work. They dug out the center of the circle. That made the floor of the earth lodge lower than the land outside.

The women then cut blocks of soil. The soil was held together by grass and roots. The women pounded the blocks to make them flat. They used the blocks to make the roof.

► **How did men and women share the work of building the earth lodge?**

_____

_____

Finally, the women dug a deep hole near the door. This hole was about eight feet deep. It was very wide at the bottom. But at the top, it was just wide enough to let a person down. The family stored food and clothing there for the winter. Look at the picture of the hole on the left.

► **Look at the picture on the right. Put an X where you could dig the hole to store food.**

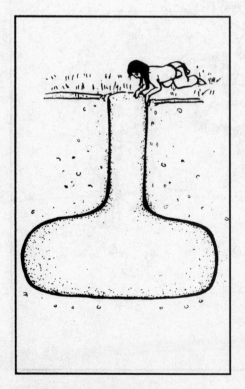

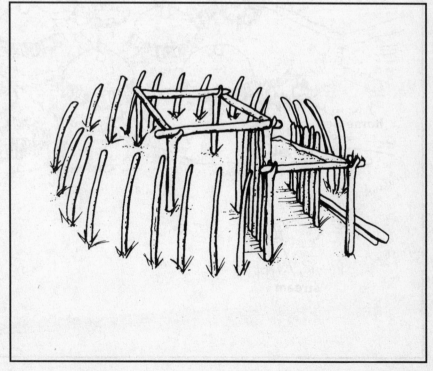

Look at the **diagram** of an Omaha village. A diagram is a drawing that shows how something works. Labels on the diagram explain the drawing.

This diagram shows how the Omaha lived. Omaha men, women, and children fished in the stream. Fields surrounded the village. Each family grew corn, beans, squash, and melons in its own field. Each family had horses, too. They were useful for hunting and traveling. Horses were very important to the Omaha.

➤ **Draw a line under the label that tells you where the Omaha farmed.**

Circle the label that tells you where the Omaha lived.

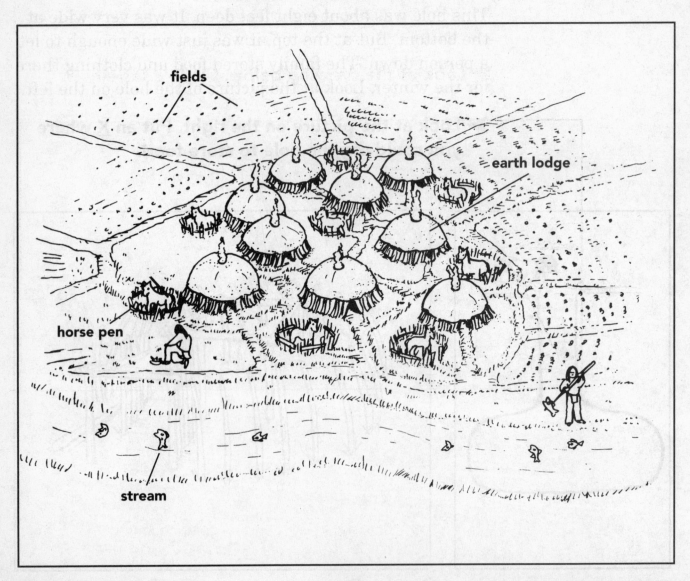

Every June, the whole Omaha village changed. Almost everybody would leave! June was the time for the buffalo hunt.

Everyone went to hunt buffalo, except the old and the sick. Most villagers packed up and headed west. That's where the buffalo lived. They wandered the plains to the west.

The Omaha often had to travel many miles to find the buffalo. They took their bows and arrows and their cooking tools.

The Omaha hunted the buffalo for food. They used the skin to make **tepees**. Tepees were the tents that the Omaha lived in when they traveled. The tepees were easy to carry from one place to another. Setting up the tepee was a woman's job. She made the tepee out of poles and buffalo skin.

▶ **Look at the drawing below. Circle a tepee.**

The men went out to hunt the buffalo. When they saw the buffalo, they got on their horses. Sometimes the Omaha had to follow the buffalo for several days before they could get close enough to the buffalo. Then they quietly made a circle around the buffalo.

With screams and shouts, the hunters moved closer to the buffalo. The frightened animals ran in circles. This gave the hunters the chance to attack them with their bows and arrows.

▶ **How did horses help the Omaha hunt? Write your answer here.**

_____

_____

Then the women went to work on the buffalo. They were careful not to waste anything. They cut up all the meat and dried some for winter. They made clothes from the skin. The women also used the skin to make blankets and shoes.

The Omaha hunted buffalo all summer. By September, they returned to their villages. September was the time to pick the corn and other crops. It was the time to fish the streams. Crops and fish could be dried and stored for the winter.

The Omaha wondered what they would find when they got back. Would everything still be there? Would the crops still be in the fields? Or had they been stolen? When that happened, winter was very hard indeed. One way or another, the Omaha had to get ready for the cold months. It was time to go home.

Name _____   Date _____

Chapter Checkup ✔

➤ **Darken the circle by the answer that best completes each sentence.**

1. The Omaha lived in what is now
Ⓐ Florida.
Ⓑ Nebraska.
Ⓒ Oregon.
Ⓓ New York.

2. An earth lodge is
Ⓐ a community center.
Ⓑ where the buffalo lived.
Ⓒ what we live in today.
Ⓓ a house that the Omaha used.

3. The Omaha used buffalo for
Ⓐ food and clothing.
Ⓑ traveling and sharing.
Ⓒ pets and food.
Ⓓ farmwork.

4. In June, everyone left the Omaha villages to hunt buffalo except the
Ⓐ women and babies.
Ⓑ children and grandparents.
Ⓒ old and sick.
Ⓓ men and teenagers.

5. The Omaha lived near
Ⓐ the Hudson River.
Ⓑ the Nile River.
Ⓒ the Missouri River.
Ⓓ Niagara Falls.

6. The Omaha made tepees from
Ⓐ buffalo skin.
Ⓑ stone.
Ⓒ cement.
Ⓓ bricks.

Thinking & Writing

Why were the buffalo important to the Omaha? Write your answer here.

_____

_____

_____

_____

_____

_____

_____

CHAPTER 13 Early Communities

About 150 years ago, a new group of people came into Omaha land. They wanted land to farm. These people were called **pioneers** because they were among the first Americans to settle in this area.

➤ **Look at the picture. Circle what the pioneers used for transportation.**

The pioneers came west from St. Louis, Missouri, in the 1850s. At that time, there were about 100,000 people in St. Louis. There were only about 2,000 Omaha people.

The pioneers took the Omaha land. They did not ask to use it. They just moved in. The Omaha knew they could not fight so many people. So they moved farther west.

In 1854, the pioneers started a town near the Missouri River. They named it after the Omaha who once lived there. Omaha was a good place for a community. It was in the center of the country. Pioneers passed through Omaha on their way west. In Omaha, they bought things they needed.

➤ **Circle Omaha on the map below.**

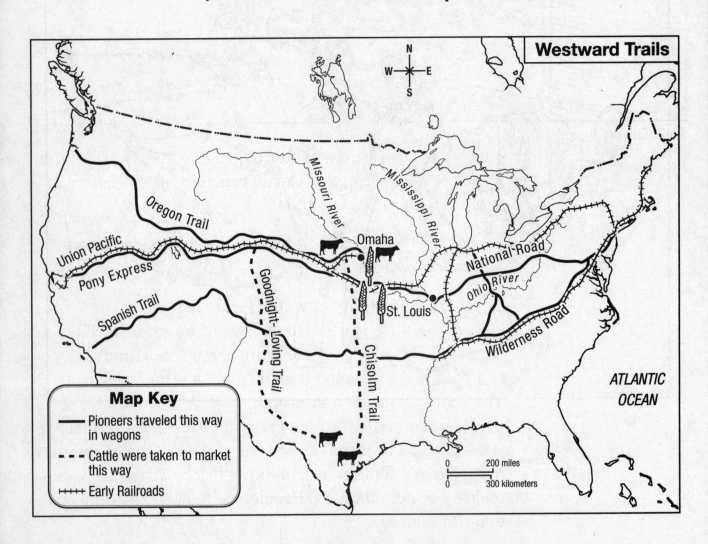

Westward Trails

Map Key
— Pioneers traveled this way in wagons
- - - Cattle were taken to market this way
++++ Early Railroads

Early Omaha had many kinds of businesses.

Omaha was in the center of good farmland. The land was good for cattle, too. Cattle ranchers and farmers sold their goods in Omaha.

▶ **Look at the picture above. Circle a place where goods were sold.**

There was plenty of water for the people of Omaha because the Missouri River was so close. The Missouri was also good for transportation. Hundreds of steamboats traveled to and from Omaha every year. They carried goods and people.

Many new **industries** grew in Omaha. An industry is a business that makes or trades goods. One of the first industries in Omaha was making bricks. Another was making wooden boards. People needed bricks and wood to build houses.

In time, more people moved to Omaha and started new businesses. Then a railroad was built that crossed the entire United States. It went right through Omaha!

Look at the **time line** below. A time line shows a number of years. Marks on the line stand for things that happened. The time line shows events in the order that they happened. This time line shows important events in Omaha's early history.

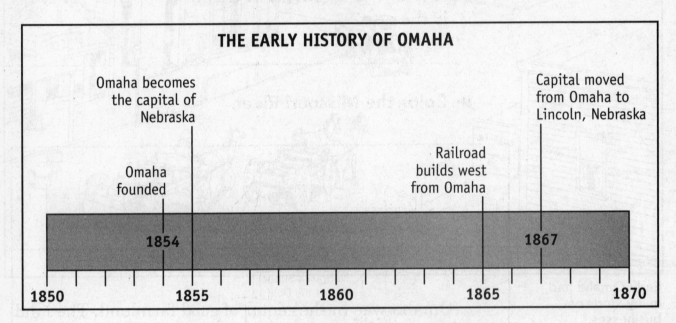

THE EARLY HISTORY OF OMAHA

Omaha becomes the capital of Nebraska

Capital moved from Omaha to Lincoln, Nebraska

Omaha founded

Railroad builds west from Omaha

1854   1867

1850   1855   1860   1865   1870

▶ **Look at the year Omaha was founded. How many years later was the railroad built?**

_____

The railroad helped Omaha grow. Trains brought cattle in from far away. Soon, new jobs opened in meatpacking, or the industry of getting meat ready to sell in other cities. Thousands of people came to Omaha for these jobs.

The trains also brought more corn and wheat from the farms. Mills were built to grind the corn and wheat into flour. The mills needed workers. So even more people came to Omaha to work in the mills.

Omaha's population grew quickly. New houses were built. New schools opened. So did a public library. Omaha grew from a tiny community into a busy city.

▶ **Look at the map of Omaha. It has a <u>grid</u>, or lines that cross each other to form squares. Each square is named with a letter and number. Put your finger on the letter C. Follow it down to row 2. The airport is in C-2. In what grid square is the zoo?**

_____

▶ **Color the Missouri River.**

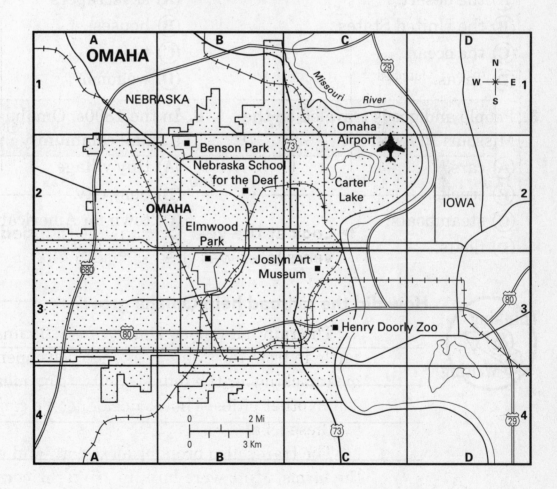

Chapter Checkup ✔

▶ **Darken the circle by the answer that best completes each sentence.**

1. The people who moved west long ago to find land were called
(A) Canadians.
(B) meatpackers.
(C) pioneers.
(D) New Yorkers.

2. Omaha is in the middle of
(A) the desert.
(B) the United States.
(C) the ocean.
(D) Texas.

3. People and goods traveled on the Missouri River in
(A) cars.
(B) trucks.
(C) steamboats.
(D) floats.

4. An industry is a business that
(A) makes or trades goods.
(B) provides services.
(C) is run by volunteers.
(D) was begun by the Omaha.

5. Bricks and wooden boards were needed in Omaha to build
(A) skyscrapers.
(B) houses.
(C) tepees.
(D) wagons.

6. In the 1800s, Omaha changed from a small community into a
(A) tiny village.
(B) busy city.
(C) town for American Indians.
(D) large state.

Thinking & Writing

How did the railroad help Omaha grow?

_____

_____

_____

_____

_____

_____

CHAPTER  14 Communities Grow

After 1880, Omaha kept growing. Today, Omaha is Nebraska's biggest city. More than 390,000 people live there.

The city keeps growing because industry keeps growing. Preparing food is still Omaha's biggest industry, and Omaha is still a railroad center. But new industries and jobs have come to the city. These include computer work and selling goods by telephone.

Trucking is also a key industry in Omaha. There are nearly 100 trucking businesses in the city. Trucking is an important way to move goods.

➤ **What is another way to move goods? Write your answer here.**

_____

Omaha, the largest city in Nebraska, is near the Missouri River.

As a city grows, it can have new problems. In parts of Omaha, some older buildings began to fall apart while other parts of the city grew. People began to move away from the older areas. As the people left, businesses in the area closed. Shoe repair shops, food stores, and other businesses could no longer make enough money. Finally, many buildings were left empty. The streets got dirty.

▶ **Look at the picture. What happens to a house when it is left empty? Write your answer here.**

_____

_____

Today, people in Omaha are building new houses. Houses that are falling apart are being torn down to make room for the new homes.

In many parts of town, old buildings are being repaired. In one part of downtown Omaha, old warehouses have been fixed up. This area is called Old Market. Some old buildings have been turned into shops. Others have become restaurants. Now the old buildings are as good as new.

➤ **Look at the picture. Has this building been fixed? How can you tell? Write your answer here.**

_____

_____

Look at the map of Omaha. It shows the community in 1854, in 1880, and today. What changes do you see? What do you think will happen to Omaha in the **future**? The future means the years to come. Do you think that more people will live in Omaha? Or do you think that fewer people will live there? What changes could new kinds of transportation and industry bring?

➤ **Look at the map. Name three ways in which Omaha has changed since 1854. Write your answer here.**

_____

_____

_____

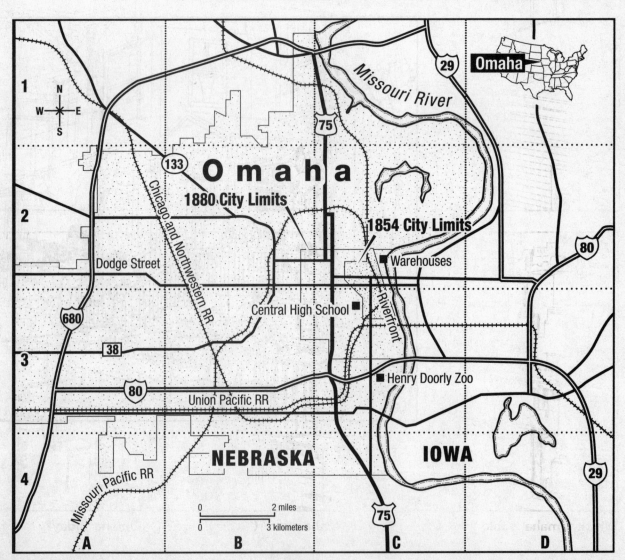

Look at the picture that shows Omaha just after it was settled. Then look at the picture of Omaha as it is today. What do you think Omaha's future will be like? Can you guess?

➤ **Name two ways that the Omaha of yesterday and the Omaha of today are different. Write your answer here.**

_____

_____

Which Omaha would you rather live in? Omaha over 100 years ago? Or Omaha today?

Chapter Checkup ✓

▶ **Darken the circle by the answer that best completes each sentence.**

1. Today, Omaha is the biggest city in
   Ⓐ Kansas.
   Ⓑ Oklahoma.
   Ⓒ Texas.
   Ⓓ Nebraska.

2. Getting food ready for sale is
   Ⓐ not important in Omaha.
   Ⓑ the biggest industry in Omaha.
   Ⓒ not important anywhere.
   Ⓓ a very small business.

3. One industry that has grown in Omaha in the last 100 years is
   Ⓐ hunting buffalo.
   Ⓑ trucking.
   Ⓒ fishing.
   Ⓓ mills.

4. When people leave one part of a city, the houses there may
   Ⓐ look cleaner.
   Ⓑ start to fall apart.
   Ⓒ get crowded.
   Ⓓ become new.

5. Since 1854, Omaha has become
   Ⓐ empty.
   Ⓑ smaller.
   Ⓒ bigger.
   Ⓓ rural.

6. The future means
   Ⓐ past years.
   Ⓑ what is happening now.
   Ⓒ the years to come.
   Ⓓ what just happened.

Thinking & Writing

Important jobs in Omaha include preparing food, computer work, and selling goods by telephone. Which job would you like the best? Explain your answer.

_____

_____

_____

_____

_____

_____

Unit 5 | Skill Builder

Using a Diagram

Not all American Indian groups lived in communities like those of the Omaha. The Tlingit American Indians lived in southeastern Alaska. The diagram shows you what a Tlingit village looked like.

➤ **Use the diagram to answer the questions.**

totem pole

wooden canoe

1. The Tlingit used trees from nearby forests to build houses called plank houses. Find the line pointing to a plank house. Add the label "plank house."

2. Circle another thing the Tlingit made out of wood.

_____

3. What two foods did the Tlingit eat?

_____

4. The Tlingit carved animal pictures in tall tree trunks. What are these carvings called?

_____

Unit 5  Review

➤ **Each sentence below has a word or words missing. Choose the missing word or words from the boxes. Then write the word or words in the correct places on the puzzle.**

ACROSS | diagram | earth lodges | industries |

1. A _____ is a picture that shows how something works.

2. The Omaha lived in homes called _____.

3. Businesses that make or trade goods are _____.

DOWN | time line | tepees | pioneers | future |

4. The _____ is all the years to come.

5. The Omaha lived in skin tents called _____ when they hunted.

6. The first American _____ came to Omaha land about 150 years ago.

7. A _____ shows events in the order that they happened.

Unit 5  Test

➤ Darken the circle by the answer that best completes each sentence.

1. The Omaha lived
   - Ⓐ in the southeastern United States.
   - Ⓑ near Lincoln, Nebraska.
   - Ⓒ near the Atlantic Ocean.
   - Ⓓ near the Missouri River.

2. The Omaha got food by
   - Ⓐ hunting and farming.
   - Ⓑ raising cattle and trading.
   - Ⓒ making bricks and boards.
   - Ⓓ meatpacking.

3. The city of Omaha grew quickly because
   - Ⓐ a new high school was built.
   - Ⓑ a railroad was built.
   - Ⓒ people thought St. Louis was too boring.
   - Ⓓ many houses were built.

4. You can see events in the order they happened on a
   - Ⓐ bar graph.
   - Ⓑ globe.
   - Ⓒ map.
   - Ⓓ time line.

5. The people who came west to Omaha about 150 years ago were
   - Ⓐ American Indians.
   - Ⓑ pioneers.
   - Ⓒ Aztecs.
   - Ⓓ Mexicans.

6. Today, many people in Omaha have
   - Ⓐ ranching jobs.
   - Ⓑ trucking jobs.
   - Ⓒ fishing jobs.
   - Ⓓ farming jobs.

If you could visit Omaha in the past, what time would you choose? Explain your answer.

_____

_____

_____

_____

_____

_____

CHAPTER 15 The U.S. Capital

One community that is important to all citizens of the United States is Washington, D.C. Washington is the capital of the United States. D.C. stands for the District of Columbia. It is land that is set aside for the nation's capital. Washington, D.C., is not part of any state.

A City of Government

The government of the United States meets in Washington, D.C. This government is called the national government. The leader of the U.S. national government is the President. The picture below shows the White House, where the U.S. President lives.

➤ **Why do you think the President lives in such a big house? Write your answer here.**

_____

_____

The U.S. President lives and works in the White House.

The Capitol is also in Washington. It's the big building in the picture below. Lawmakers from all the states meet in this building.

Like the lawmakers who are part of community government, these lawmakers are **elected**. To elect someone means to choose that person by voting. Lawmakers are elected by the people who live in their state.

All the lawmakers elected by the states meet and work together in the Capitol building. This group of lawmakers is called **Congress**.

➤ **Write *Capitol* on the picture next to the Capitol building.**

Next to the picture, write the name of the group that meets in the Capitol.

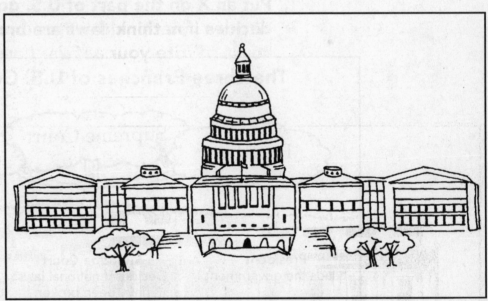

The Capitol is one of the most famous buildings in Washington, D.C.

The **Supreme Court** building is near the Capitol in Washington, D.C. The Supreme Court judges meet here. These judges are called justices. The Supreme Court is the most important U.S. court. It decides things about the laws of the United States. Everyone must follow what the Supreme Court justices decide about the U.S. laws.

The President, Congress, and Supreme Court form the three branches, or parts, of the U.S. government. The chart shows these parts. A chart shows information in a way that is easy to read.

▶ **Underline the part of government that makes laws that all U.S. states have to follow.**

Circle the part of government that leads the U.S. government.

Put an X on the part of U.S. government that decides if national laws are broken.

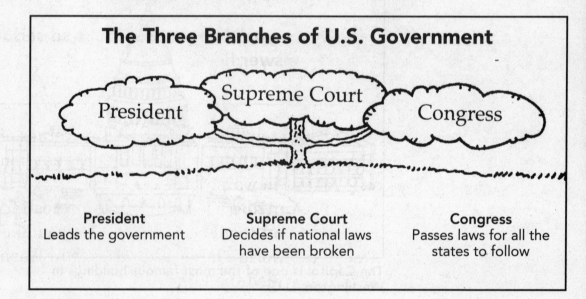

The Three Branches of U.S. Government

President	Supreme Court	Congress
Leads the government	Decides if national laws have been broken	Passes laws for all the states to follow

The statue of Abraham Lincoln is in the Lincoln Memorial.

How did Washington, D.C., get its name? That's easy! It was named after George Washington, the first President of the United States.

The picture above shows another President. His name was Abraham Lincoln. Lincoln was one of the most important U.S. Presidents. He was the President who ended slavery in the United States.

➤ **Why do you think Lincoln looks so serious? Write your answer here.**

_____

Washington has many beautiful statues of Presidents. It also has many statues that honor people who fought in wars.

Washington has many other interesting places that are important to all U.S. citizens. Do you like books? One of the world's largest libraries is in Washington, D.C. It is called the Library of Congress.

The Wright brothers' airplane

Gemini space capsule

Washington is also home to a very famous museum. Its name is the Smithsonian Institution. But its nickname is "the nation's attic." This museum is made up of eight museums. Together they hold many treasures that belong to the people of the United States. Among these treasures are toys and games used by U.S. children long ago. The museums also hold the first airplane made by the Wright brothers and the Gemini spacecraft that went to the moon!

▶ **Why do you think the things shown here should be stored in Washington, D.C.?**

_____

_____

_____

The original building of the Smithsonian Institute is nicknamed "the castle."

Chapter Checkup ✓

➤ **Darken the circle by the answer that best completes each sentence.**

1. The District of Columbia is
  Ⓐ part of another country.
  Ⓑ the name of a U.S. state.
  Ⓒ an area for the U.S. capital.
  Ⓓ the highest court in the land.

2. The White House is where
  Ⓐ people in Congress work.
  Ⓑ the President lives and works.
  Ⓒ old U.S. things are kept.
  Ⓓ the Supreme Court meets.

3. Congress meets in the
  Ⓐ Supreme Court building.
  Ⓑ Capitol.
  Ⓒ Lincoln Memorial.
  Ⓓ Smithsonian Institution.

4. Elected means
  Ⓐ serves for life.
  Ⓑ chosen by the President.
  Ⓒ chosen by a vote.
  Ⓓ ruled by law.

5. The Supreme Court decides
  Ⓐ if national laws are broken.
  Ⓑ where to put statues.
  Ⓒ what new places to build.
  Ⓓ what money to print.

6. The national government is made up of
  Ⓐ two parts.
  Ⓑ four parts.
  Ⓒ eight parts.
  Ⓓ three parts.

Thinking & Writing

How are the national government and community governments alike? Write your answer here.

_____

_____

_____

_____

_____

_____

_____

111

CHAPTER 16 Communities Celebrate

U.S. communities **celebrate** many of the same holidays. To celebrate means to remember an important day or event in a special way. Can you think of some holidays you celebrate with your family?

National Holidays

Each year in November, people in every city and town in the United States sit down to a big dinner. This is a holiday people in the United States call Thanksgiving.

The first Thanksgiving was held in 1621 by Pilgrims who were new to America. They gave thanks for good crops and for being alive. They feasted for three days. They ate foods such as turkey, deer, eel, dried berries, corn, and pumpkin.

➤ **What foods did the Pilgrims eat that you eat? Write your answer here.**

_____

_____

Some of the people at the first Thanksgiving were friendly neighbors. They included an American Indian chief and many other American Indians. They had helped the Pilgrims stay alive. The American Indians taught the Pilgrims how to grow corn. They showed them how to fish with a spear.

Unit 6, Chapter 16
Core Skills Social Studies 3, SV 9781419034251

The idea of spending a holiday together became a U.S. **tradition**. A tradition is something people do in the same way that has been passed down over many years.

In 1863, President Abraham Lincoln made Thanksgiving more than a tradition. He made it a national holiday for everyone in the United States.

➤ **How is your celebration different from the Thanksgiving in the picture below? Write your answer here.**

_____

_____

On July 4, 1776, another U.S. tradition began. On that day, the United States first called itself a free nation. The people fought a long war so they would no longer be ruled by Great Britain. After the war, people began to celebrate with speeches, parades, and parties. Today, this holiday is known as the Fourth of July. Many communities celebrate the birthday of the United States with fireworks and parades. Their celebrations honor U.S. citizens' freedoms.

The flag is an important part of the Fourth of July celebration. The U.S. flag has 50 stars, one for each state. In this way, the flag stands for the fact that we are a single nation made up of many states.

➤ **Look at the pictures. Circle the U.S. flag.**

Why do you think this might be a Fourth of July parade?

_____

_____

Other Community Celebrations

Citizens of the United States are free to enjoy their own family traditions along with U.S. traditions. Your own traditions include many things. One might be the language your family speaks. Another might be the kind of church your family goes to. Still another can be the special holidays you celebrate.

The picture below shows a giant paper dragon leading a parade. The dragon stands for strength and goodness. The parade is a big part of the Chinese New Year celebration. This special holiday usually takes place in February. The parade lasts three hours. It is colorful and noisy as people toss little firecrackers into the street. Many people who came from China now live in communities in the United States. They celebrate their new year in this traditional way.

▶ **Put an X on the man who is wearing the dragon mask.**

In Chinese tradition, the dragon is seen as a protector.

115

The picture below shows men taking part in a **fiesta** in San Antonio, Texas. *Fiesta* is the Spanish word for "holiday." Many people in Texas came from Mexico. This fiesta honors people whose families are Mexican.

➤ **Circle the Mexican hats.**

Many other groups of people in the United States have special celebrations, too. Thousands of people from Vietnam have settled in the United States. Vietnam is a country in Asia. Vietnamese people celebrate a special children's holiday in August or September. This celebration is called Trung Thu. During this celebration, children walk through their community carrying little lamps and singing songs. People give the children special cakes, cookies, and candy.

Traditional costumes help people celebrate a fiesta.

Chapter Checkup ✓

▶ **Darken the circle by the answer that best completes each sentence.**

1. The Pilgrims held Thanksgiving so they could
   Ⓐ help the American Indians.
   Ⓑ start an American tradition.
   Ⓒ get to know their neighbors better.
   Ⓓ give thanks for good crops.

2. Something people do in the same way that has been passed down over many years is
   Ⓐ a parade.
   Ⓑ a holiday.
   Ⓒ a tradition.
   Ⓓ a celebration.

3. President Lincoln made Thanksgiving a
   Ⓐ national tradition.
   Ⓑ national holiday.
   Ⓒ friendly meal.
   Ⓓ national birthday.

4. The Fourth of July celebrates
   Ⓐ parties and parades.
   Ⓑ the parades of 1776.
   Ⓒ Chinese New Year.
   Ⓓ the birthday of the United States.

5. Two things that can be part of your own family's tradition are
   Ⓐ language and holidays.
   Ⓑ animals and television.
   Ⓒ harvests and dragons.
   Ⓓ parents and meetings.

6. A fiesta is a
   Ⓐ holiday.
   Ⓑ poem.
   Ⓒ parade.
   Ⓓ speech.

Thinking & Writing

How do national places and holidays help us feel like Americans? Write your answer here.

_____

_____

_____

_____

Name _____   Date _____

Using a Chart

➤ Did you know that there are thousands of celebrations and festivals in the United States? Look at the chart below to find out when, where, why, and how some other communities celebrate. Use the chart to answer the questions.

Community Celebrations

	Koloa Plantation Days	Chasco Fiesta	Tulip Festival	Cherry Festival
When?	July	March	April	July
Where?	Koloa Town, Kauai, Hawaii	New Port Richey, Florida	Owensville, Missouri	Traverse City, Michigan
Why?	Celebrates the first planting in the late 1800s of sugar crops in Hawaii	Celebrates the friendship of Calusa Indians and Spanish settlers	Celebrates the beginning of spring	Celebrates that the area's cherry crops are ripe and ready for eating
How?	A parade, games, and a car show	Games, dances, and food	A quilt show, a dance, and a flower show	A parade, pie-eating contest, music, and the crowning of the National Cherry Queen

1. Which celebration is about friendship?

_____

2. What festival could you see in Missouri in April?

_____

3. What community would you be in if you entered a cherry pie-eating contest?

_____

4. Which two celebrations honor crops?

_____

Unit 6  Review

▶ **Use a word from the box to complete each sentence below. Write the word on the lines next to each sentence.**

| celebrate | elected | fiesta | Congress | flag | President | tradition |

1. Lawmakers from every state make up ____.

☐ _ _ _ _ _ _ _

2. A ____ is something people do in the same way that has been passed down over many years.

_ _ ☐ _ _ _ _ _ _

3. The ____, Congress, and Supreme Court form the three branches of U.S. government.

☐ _ _ _ _ _ _ _ _

4. In Spanish, a holiday is called a ____.

_ ☐ _ _ _ _

5. National lawmakers are ____ or chosen, by voting.

_ _ _ _ ☐ _ _

6. To remember an important day or event is to ____ .

_ _ _ _ _ _ ☐ _ _

7. The U.S. ____ has 50 stars, one for each state.

☐ _ _ _

▶ **Use the letters in the boxes to answer the following riddle.**

Riddle: I am a place in the United States, but I am not in any of the 50 states. What am I ?

Answer: The _ _ _ _ _ _ _ _

Unit 6  Test

➤ **Darken the circle by the answer that best completes each sentence.**

1. The President and Congress are part of the
   - Ⓐ state government.
   - Ⓑ national government.
   - Ⓒ Supreme Court.
   - Ⓓ Smithsonian Institution.

2. Members of Congress
   - Ⓐ make laws for the whole country.
   - Ⓑ set up statues to honor soldiers.
   - Ⓒ decide if a national law is broken.
   - Ⓓ work in the White House.

3. Members of the Supreme Court are called
   - Ⓐ governors.
   - Ⓑ branches.
   - Ⓒ presidents.
   - Ⓓ justices.

4. When people do something in the same way that has been passed down over many years, they are following a
   - Ⓐ holiday.
   - Ⓑ tradition.
   - Ⓒ freedom.
   - Ⓓ family.

5. Two national holidays are
   - Ⓐ fiesta and Chinese New Year.
   - Ⓑ the Cherry Festival and New Year's Eve.
   - Ⓒ the last day of school and Christmas.
   - Ⓓ the Fourth of July and Thanksgiving.

6. Dragons are often a part of
   - Ⓐ Thanksgiving.
   - Ⓑ Thu Trung.
   - Ⓒ Juneteenth.
   - Ⓓ Chinese New Year.

Would you rather work as the President, a member of Congress, or a justice on the Supreme Court? Give reasons for your answer.

_____

_____

_____

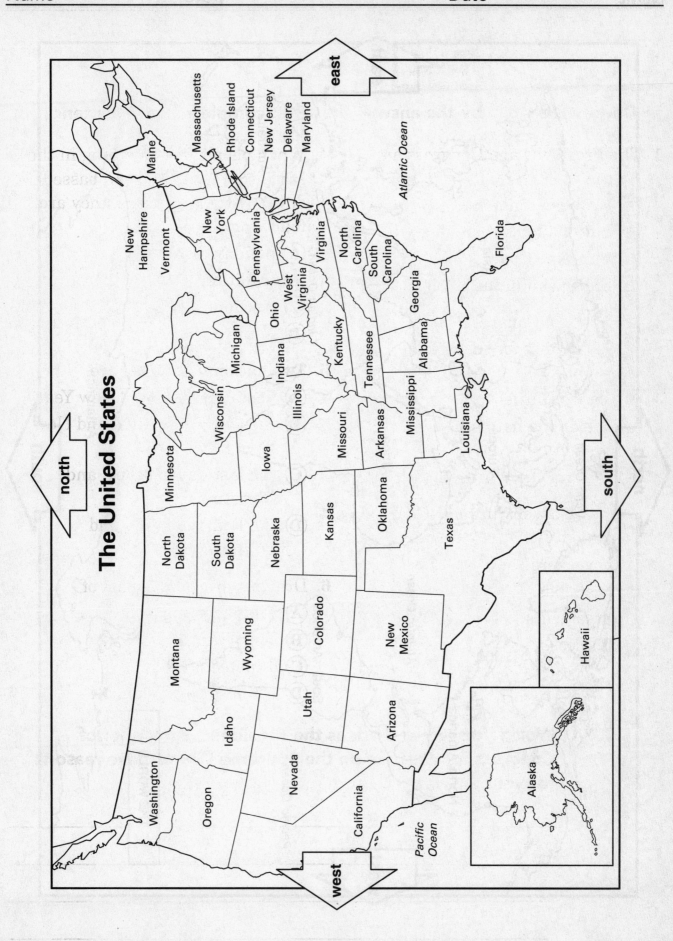

The United States

north

east

south

west

Massachusetts
Rhode Island
Connecticut
New Jersey
Delaware
Maryland

Maine

New Hampshire
Vermont

New York

Pennsylvania

West Virginia

Virginia

Virginia

North Carolina

South Carolina

Georgia

Florida

Atlantic Ocean

Ohio

Michigan

Indiana

Illinois

Kentucky

Tennessee

Alabama

Mississippi

Wisconsin

Minnesota

Iowa

Missouri

Arkansas

Louisiana

North Dakota

South Dakota

Nebraska

Kansas

Oklahoma

Texas

Montana

Wyoming

Colorado

New Mexico

Idaho

Utah

Arizona

Washington

Oregon

Nevada

California

Pacific Ocean

Hawaii

Alaska

United States Map
Core Skills Social Studies 3, SV 9781419034251

Name _____   Date _____

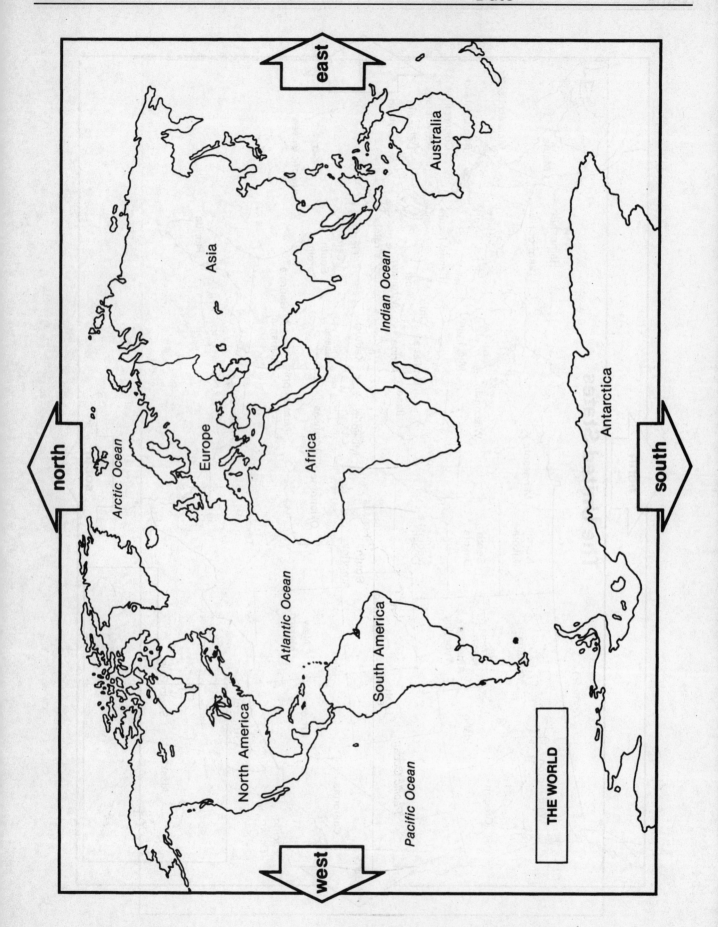

Core Skills Social Studies 3, SV 9781419034251

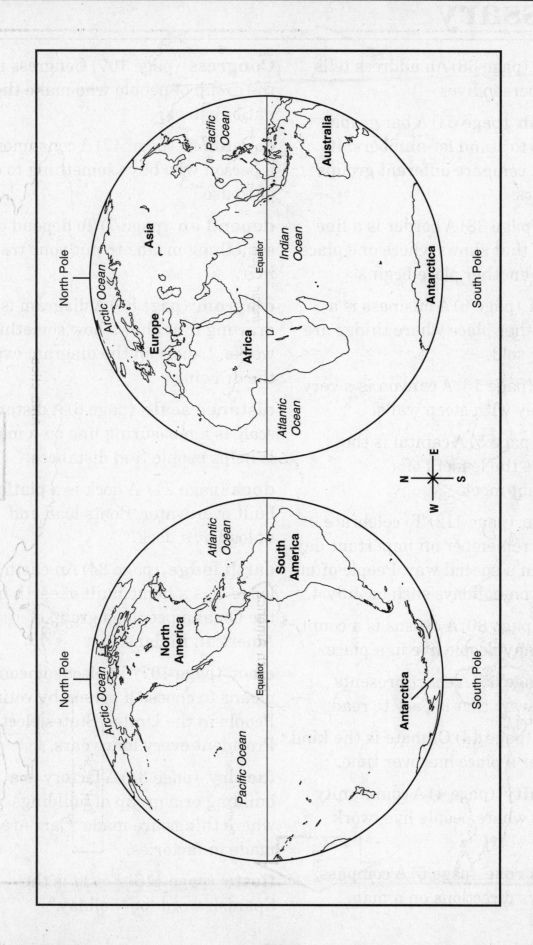

Glossary

address (page 38) An address tells where a person lives.

bar graph (page 63) A bar graph uses bars to stand for numbers. It helps you compare different groups of numbers.

border (page 38) A border is a line on a map that shows where one place ends and another place begins.

business (page 8) A business is a store or other place where things are bought or sold.

canyon (page 16) A canyon is a very deep valley with steep walls.

capital (page 5) A capital is the city where the leaders of a government meet.

celebrate (page 112) To celebrate means to remember an important day or event in a special way. People often celebrate on holidays such as July 4.

census (page 80) A census is a count of how many people live in a place.

chart (page 65) A chart presents facts in a way that is easy to read.

climate (page 14) Climate is the kind of weather a place has over time.

community (page 4) A community is a place where people live, work, and play.

compass rose (page 5) A compass rose shows directions on a map.

Congress (page 107) Congress is the group of people who make the nation's laws.

consumer (page 47) A consumer is a person who buys something to eat or to use.

depend on (page 7) To depend on something means to put your trust in it.

diagram (page 86) A diagram is a drawing that shows how something works. Labels on the diagram explain the drawing.

distance scale (page 6) A distance scale is a measuring line on a map. It helps people find distances.

dock (page 21) A dock is a platform built over water. Boats load and unload at a dock.

earth lodge (page 84) An earth lodge was a home built of earth by the Omaha people, a group of American Indians.

elect (page 107) To elect someone means to choose a person by voting. People in the United States elect a President every four years.

factory (page 34) A factory is a building or a group of buildings where things are made. Cars are made in factories.

fiesta (page 116) *Fiesta* is the Spanish word for "holiday."

flowchart (page 54) A flowchart is a diagram that shows the step-by-step order in which something is done.

future (page 100) The future means the time that is to come.

globe (page 57) A globe is a round model of Earth.

goods (page 34) Goods are things that are made to be sold, such as shoes or toys.

government (page 64) A government is a group of leaders who make laws.

grid (page 95) A grid is a group of lines that cross each other to form squares. Each square is named with a letter and number.

harbor (page 33) A harbor is an area of water that is protected from wind and strong waves. It is a safe place for ships.

industry (page 93) An industry is a business that makes or trades goods.

judge (page 64) A judge decides if a law has been broken.

landform (page 15) A landform is a shape of the land, such as a mountain or a hill.

law (page 64) A law is a rule made by a government.

lawmakers (page 64) Lawmakers are people who make new laws and change old ones.

map key (page 5) A map key tells about each symbol on a map. It tells what each symbol stands for.

mayor (page 64) A mayor is a person who leads a community.

mineral (page 13) A mineral is something made by nature that you can usually find in the earth in rocks.

mountain (page 15) A mountain is very high land.

natural resource (page 12) A natural resource is something from nature that people need and use. Water and trees are natural resources.

needs (page 46) Needs are things people must have in order to live.

pioneer (page 91) A pioneer is a person who goes to live in a new place. Many pioneers went west to farm the land.

plain (page 15) A plain is flat land.

political map (page 38) A political map of the United States shows states and their borders.

population (page 23) Population is the number of people living in a place.

producer (page 47) A producer is someone who gets paid for growing or for making something.

public (page 9) A public place is a place for everyone to use.

rural (page 23) A rural area is in the country. Farms are found in rural areas.

service (page 48) A service is something people do that other people need or want.

shelter (page 46) Shelter is a home or a place to live.

suburb (page 27) A suburb is a community near a big city.

Supreme Court (page 108) The Supreme Court is the most important court in the United States.

symbol (page 5) A symbol is found on a map. A symbol stands for a real thing.

tax (page 75) A tax is money that people pay to the government.

tepee (page 87) A tepee was a tent made from buffalo skin. The Omaha people lived in tepees when they traveled to hunt buffalo.

time line (page 94) A time line shows a number of years. Marks on the line stand for things that happened. The time line shows the order in which things happened.

tradition (page 113) A tradition is something people do in the same way that has been passed down over many years.

transportation (page 29) Transportation is how people or things get from one place to another.

valley (page 16) A valley is the low land between hills or mountains.

volunteer (page 24) A volunteer is a person who is not paid for his or her work.

wants (page 46) Wants are things people would like but do not need to have in order to live.

weather (page 11) Weather is how hot or cold and how wet or dry it is.

Core Skills Social Studies 3, SV 9781419034251

Answer Key

NOTE: For answers not provided, check that students have given an appropriate response and/or followed the directions given.

page 6
About 1 ½ miles

page 10
1. B   2. B   3. D   4. A   5. C   6. D
Answers will vary.

page 17
1. B   2. D   3. A   4. D   5. C   6. B
Answers will vary.

page 18
1. mountains and plains
2. Students should correctly identify plains and mountains.
3. Olympia
4. It is flat; it is made up of plains.

page 19
1. community   2. business   3. plain
4. landform   5. minerals   6. public
7. symbol

page 20
1. B   2. A   3. C   4. D   5. B   6. D
Answers will vary.

page 26
1. D   2. C   3. A   4. D   5. C   6. B
Answers will vary.

page 31
1. B   2. A   3. C   4. B   5. B   6. D
Answers will vary.

page 36
1. D   2. A   3. C   4. D   5. C   6. B
Answers will vary.

page 42
1. C   2. B   3. A   4. B   5. D   6. B
Answers will vary.

page 43
1. circle the river symbol
2. trace the Yukon River path
3. circle Juneau
4. Arctic Ocean
5. Canada

page 44
1. factories   2. suburbs   3. transportation
4. population   5. volunteers
RURAL

page 45
1. B   2. D   3. B   4. C   5. B   6. A
Answers will vary.

page 46
want

page 49
Clean water helps people from getting sick.

page 52
1. A   2. C   3. C   4. B   5. D   6. B
Answers will vary.

page 58
1. B   2. B   3. D   4. C   5. B   6. C
Answers will vary.

page 59
1. circle the carwash
2. underline the children eating pizza
3. the man with the clean car
4. A want; he didn't need to have his car washed to live.

page 60
1. consumer   2. producer   3. shelter
4. service   5. flowchart   6. needs
7. globe

page 61
1. D   2. C   3. B   4. C   5. D   6. A
Answers will vary.

page 63

people running for class leader

number of votes

10; 8; circle Brandon

page 66

1. D   **2.** C   **3.** A   **4.** D   **5.** D   **6.** B

Answers will vary.

page 69

35 miles per hour

page 72

1. B   **2.** D   **3.** C   **4.** A   **5.** C   **6.** B

Answers will vary.

page 78

In picture A, a thief is breaking into a store. Students should make the following line connections: A-4; B-2; C-3; D-1.

page 79

1. C   **2.** B   **3.** D   **4.** A   **5.** B   **6.** D

Answers will vary.

page 80

1. 5,000

2. 1990

3. between 1980 and 1990

4. The census shows that the population of Blue Bay decreased.

page 81

1. laws   **2.** census   **3.** bar

4. judge   **5.** government   **6.** mayor

7. service

LEADERS

page 82

1. B   **2.** D   **3.** A   **4.** A   **5.** C   **6.** D

Answers will vary.

page 83

It was roughly 750 miles across Omaha land.

page 90

1. B   **2.** D   **3.** A   **4.** C   **5.** C   **6.** A

Answers will vary.

page 94

11 years

page 95

C-3

page 96

1. C   **2.** B   **3.** C   **4.** A   **5.** B   **6.** B

Answers will vary.

page 102

1. D   **2.** B   **3.** B   **4.** B   **5.** C   **6.** C

Answers will vary.

page 103

1. add the label to the plank house

2. circle the totem pole, plank houses, or canoe

3. fish and deer meat

4. totem poles

page 104

1. diagram   **2.** earth lodges   **3.** industries

4. future   **5.** tepees   **6.** pioneers

7. time line

page 105

1. D   **2.** A   **3.** B   **4.** D   **5.** B   **6.** B

Answers will vary.

page 111

1. C   **2.** B   **3.** B   **4.** C   **5.** A   **6.** D

Answers will vary.

page 117

1. D   **2.** C   **3.** B   **4.** D   **5.** A   **6.** A

Answers will vary.

page 118

1. Chasco Fiesta

2. Tulip Festival

3. Traverse City, Michigan

4. Koloa Plantation Days and the Cherry Festival

page 119

1. Congress   **2.** tradition   **3.** President

4. fiesta   **5.** elected   **6.** celebrate

7. flag

CAPITAL

page 120

1. B   **2.** A   **3.** D   **4.** B   **5.** D   **6.** D

Answers will vary.

Core Skills Social Studies 3, SV 9781419034251